THE
CHINESE
AMERICANS

In a scene photographed around 1912, American flags fly in New York City's Chinatown. (LIBRARY OF CONGRESS)

THE CHINESE AMERICANS

華僑

by **MILTON MELTZER**

Illustrated with Photographs

Thomas Y. Crowell   New York

Library of Congress Cataloging in Publication Data
Meltzer, Milton, 1915–
The Chinese Americans.

Bibliography: p.
Includes index.
SUMMARY: Traces the history of the Chinese in the
United States, describing their contributions to the
development of this country and their struggle for
economic and social equality.
1. Chinese Americans—History—Juvenile literature.
[1. Chinese Americans—History] I. Title.
E184.C5M43 1980 973'.04951 79-3419
ISBN 0-690-04038-5
ISBN 0-690-04039-3 lib. bdg.

1   2   3   4   5   6   7   8   9   10
First Edition

Contents

What's Wrong with This Picture?

華僑

OPPOSITE IS AN engraving of a photograph taken over 100 years ago. It is one of the most famous pictures in American history books. The scene is a place in Utah called Promontory Point. On the day this picture was taken—May 10, 1869—Chinese construction crews of the Central Pacific Railroad, coming from the west, and Irish construction crews of the Union Pacific Railroad, coming from the east, completed the first railroad to span the North American continent.

Workers had put the last tie in place, had laid down the last rail, and had rammed home the last spike—the golden spike. The engines of the two companies that had built the transcontinental railroad moved forward until they touched.

The people who had planned the railroad, raised the money for it, and supervised the gigantic job of building it crowded in to have the official photograph taken. The workers standing on the locomotives pulled out their bottles to celebrate, and the photographer took his picture.

But something is wrong with this picture.

Look closely at the faces in it.

Nowhere can you see a Chinese person.

Yet no group of workers did more to build that railroad than the Chinese. Their bone, their muscle, their nerve, their sweat, their skill made an impossible dream come true.

One hundred years later, in 1969, America celebrated the anniversary of the completion of the railroad.

The U.S. Secretary of Transportation, speaking for himself and the President, gave a speech in honor of the magnificent achievement.

But he never mentioned the Chinese-American workers.

The Missing Men: They Built the Railroad

華僑

FOR SEVERAL YEARS, thousands of Chinese and Irish workers labored through mountain snow and desert sand to complete the transcontinental railroad.

It was the most dramatic chapter in the conquest of America's last frontier. The railroad was the only way to bridge the vast distance between the settled East and the almost empty West. Stagecoach and covered wagon straggled across trails with passengers and supplies, but they took an eternity to reach their destinations and were never sure to arrive. Congress finally agreed that a transcontinental railroad must be built, and provided for two companies to do the job. The Union Pacific would build westward from the last station at Omaha, Nebraska, and the Central Pacific, eastward from Sacramento, California. Each would be subsidized by generous land grants and loans.

Fabulous profits could be made through land deals and construction. Swarms of businessmen buzzed around the project, eager to share in the booty. Land, forests, mineral deposits, harbor rights, and franchises wound up in the hands of a small group of powerful men. "The enterprise is an inexhaustible gold mine," one of them said. Using all their skills in manipulating money and lawmakers, they built the entire railroad without using a dollar of their own.

The Central Pacific began work on the western end of the railroad at Sacramento early in 1863—a few days after President Lincoln issued the Emancipation Proclamation, in fact. Handling the vast construction project was Charles Crocker, one of the "California Quartet" who ran the Central Pacific. Crocker, a former peddler, ironworker, and gold miner, was a huge squat man who roared up and down the track like a mad bull. His work crews were young Irish immigrants arriving in San Francisco by the shipload from their poor, famine-struck homeland.

The men had to cut through the rugged mountains of the Sierra Nevada, which climbed from nearly sea level to a height of over 7,000 feet within 100 miles. In the first two years they completed only 50 miles of track. In the early 1860s there were few mechanical aids for heavy construction—no gasoline engines, no electrical power, no derricks, no tractors, not even horse-drawn scrapers or levelers. Handcart, mule cart, and human muscle with pick and shovel did the work. Gunpowder was used for blasting. To rush construction under such conditions, large crews of men had to be hired. Yet in the California of the 1860s, nothing was harder to find than labor.

As Crocker drove deeper into the hard granite of the Sierra, many of the workers quit. It got harder and harder to find replacements. White workers preferred mining or farming to carving a railroad out of granite cliffs. When advertising for 5,000 laborers produced only 1,000 men, Crocker decided to try the Chinese as laborers. They had begun immigrating to California a dozen years earlier at the time of the Gold Rush.

Crocker's construction boss, J. H. Strobridge, a tough Vermonter of Irish ancestry, bitterly opposed hiring Chinese workers. They were too small, he said; most of them weighed scarcely 100 pounds. Besides, he told Crocker, they were not masons. But Crocker reminded him that Chinese workers had built the longest stretch of masonry in the world—the Great Wall of China.

Reluctantly, Strobridge took on 50 Chinese. They were hungry for work. Many of them had been driven out of the California goldfields by the whites. Hiring them on a trial basis, Strobridge first set them to filling hand trucks with dirt, which they managed easily. Then he tested them with pick and shovel, and they did that work well, too. By the fall of 1865, Strobridge had hired 3,000 Chinese, and his agents were scouring California for more. Soon Crocker was advertising in far-off Canton for Chinese to come build the railroad.

The Chinese were trained by the Central Pacific for every kind of work, and were found to be thoroughly reliable. As their numbers grew and their skills developed, the tracks moved faster and faster up the steep slopes of the Sierra. Soon there were 12,000 Chinese on the job — nine out of ten workers were Chinese.

The Chinese worked in gangs of 12 to 20 men. Working hours were from sunrise to sunset, a day of 12 or more hours (a workday longer than the whites') under the grinding pressure of bosses yelling, "Hurry! Hurry! Hurry!"

An Irishman was in charge of each work gang.

But the Chinese chose their own "headman" to keep track of their time and to collect and divide their wages among the group. The headman also bought the provisions the gang ate and divided the cost among them at the end of each month. (White laborers got their food as part of their contracts.) In the beginning, the Chinese were paid $1 a workday, or $26 a month. (Lower pay than the whites'.) Later, pay was raised to $30 and finally to $35 a month, achieving the same rate as whites. But unlike the whites, who were given food and housing in addition to their pay, the Chinese had to feed and house themselves. This saved the Central Pacific enough money to make the cost of hiring Chinese labor about two-thirds the price of unskilled white labor. The railroad made even more profit on the Chinese because it often used them to do skilled labor—such as masonry, tracklaying, blacksmithing, and handling explosives. Whites with such skills were paid not a dollar a day but three to five dollars a day. Without figuring in this last factor, the Central Pacific in three years saved about $5.5 millions by hiring Chinese instead of white unskilled labor,

Each gang had a Chinese cook to prepare the meals. He fed them a familiar menu prepared with supplies imported from China and stored in

Pushing eastward from California toward Utah, the Central Pacific's Chinese laborers bridged many of the High Sierra chasms with timber trestles. (SOUTHERN PACIFIC TRANSPORTATION COMPANY)

a railroad car at the end of the track. The fare included dried oysters, abalone and cuttlefish, dried bamboo sprouts and mushrooms, five kinds of vegetables, pork, poultry (on holidays), vermicelli, rice, salted cabbage, dried seaweed, sweet rice crackers, sugar, four kinds of dried fruit, bacon, peanut oil, and tea. It was a varied and balanced diet. By contrast, the white workers lived on beef, beans, bread, and potatoes. On the job, to relieve their thirst, the Chinese drank warm tea toted along the track in big barrels. It was always on tap; one of the cook's chores was to see that the barrels always contained fresh tea. The whites swigged cold water—water often so dirty it made them sick. Tea was made with boiled water, and boiling killed any germs.

The Chinese cook had another duty: to have a large boiler of hot water ready each night when the men came off the job. They would sponge themselves down and change into clean clothes before eating.

The Central Pacific provided the Chinese crews with low cloth tents for housing. Many, however, preferred to live in dugouts they made themselves. The Chinese wore blue cotton smocks and trousers and broad-brimmed basket

A Chinese laborers' camp adjacent to the Central Pacific rails near Brown's Station, Nevada. (SOUTHERN PACIFIC TRANSPORTATION COMPANY)

High in the Sierra Nevada mountáins, this Chinese crewman for the Central Pacific Railroad carries barrels of warm tea for his fellow laborers. (SOUTHERN PACIFIC TRANSPORTATION COMPANY)

hats, and American boots bought at the company commissary.

In the fall of 1865, the Chinese began the attack upon a huge mountain called Cape Horn. Against its side they had to build a graded, winding roadbed for the track. They chopped and shoveled their way around the face of the massive granite wall. When there was no longer any surface for them to stand on, they were swung out into empty space by ropes suspended from the cliff high above. With hammers and hand drills they made holes in the sheer rock, tamped in gunpowder, and set fuses. Hoisted out of danger, they fired the blast, and with a great roar tons of rock and earth tumbled down the slope. Foot by foot they notched out the narrow shelf, climbing some 2,000 feet above the river tumbling below. With painful slowness the railhead was pushed on, past little mining towns with names like Gold Run, Red Dog, You Bet, and Little York. In the spring of 1866 above Dutch Flat, the heavy work of boring tunnels through the mountain began. It took five months to go the fifteen miles to Cisco, 6,000 feet above sea level. With winter just ahead, they faced deep gorges and thickly timbered ridges.

Most of the tunneling was to be done in this stretch of terrain.

That winter of 1865–66, the snow fell early. Storm after storm blew up—44 of them—making it the worst winter in many years. The Chinese worked in snow up to their knees, then to their waists, pausing only in howling gales.

Half the work force, now 10,000 men, shoveled snow to bare the ground for the grading crews. When the snow overcame them, they moved into tunnel work. The rock rubble they made by drilling and blasting had to be passed from hand to hand and piled in dumps outside the tunnels. In February, a four-day blizzard roared in, stopping all work. Then, for five days, gale winds piled the snow into drifts 60 feet deep. For another five days, snow again, ten feet more of it falling. Locomotives were ganged up to push snowplows through the drifts and to pull supply trains after them. When the trains stalled, regiments of Chinese snow shovelers had to dig them out.

With weather so bad, dugouts could not be made. The tents were feeble protection against the relentless weather, and the suffering and privation seemed endless. On the job, avalanches of snow were a constant threat. One reporter told of a snowslide engulfing two Chinese workers. "See-

*A Chinese laborer stands in front of a snowplow used by the Central
Pacific Railroad in the California mountains.* (SOUTHERN PACIFIC
TRANSPORTATION COMPANY)

ing it approach, they stepped behind a tall rock, but it buried them 50 feet deep. In spring their bodies were found standing upright, with shovels in their hands."

There were greater disasters. Snowbanks massed on the crags above Donner Pass began to slide. Thousands of tons of earth and rock came smashing down without warning. A 20-man Chinese crew was caught in the open near the entrance of Tunnel Number 9. It was the winter's worst killing; none survived. Again and again, Chinese workers were killed by blizzards and avalanches.

Three shifts of men working day and night pushed the tunnels through. The biggest of the tunnels, at the summit of the Sierra, was yet to be tackled. That winter, about 8,000 men began to hand carve their way into Tunnel Number 6. When spring came, there were still 15 feet of snow. As it began to melt, slides swept away bunkhouses, tents, and trestles. But the work went on. "The Chinese," wrote an engineer assigned to the tunneling, "were as steady, hard-working a set of men as could be found."

At the top of the Sierra, the granite proved to be harder than anyone had guessed. Cast-iron drills boring into it were blunted and broken.

Gunpowder charges scarcely made a dent in the rock. The Chinese multiplied their charges but cleared only seven inches in a day. They labored in near darkness and foul air. "Conditions grew so bad no white man would have endured them," wrote one historian. Crocker was desperate to end the costly delay. He decided to try nitroglycerine. It had much greater blasting power than gunpowder, but it was unpredictable and therefore very dangerous. Nevertheless, he ordered the Chinese to try the explosive liquid in their drill holes.

The men cut and set their fuses, ran for shelter, and waited nervously. The first blast shook the earth, smashing the stubborn granite into bits and pieces. The trouble was, the men couldn't tell if all the nitroglycerine had exploded. The first worker to slam his pick into a patch of spilled nitroglycerine, said a reporter, "was disintegrated with a flash and a roar into fiery nothingness, and most of his fellows in the vicinity along with him." But Crocker went right on using the new explosive. Only when Strobridge lost an eye to a flying chunk of granite did Crocker order the men to bury the nitroglycerine. They went back to using gunpowder.

A strange aspect of this story is that at that time

the steam drill had been developed to the point where it would have helped enormously. Crocker, of course, knew all about it. But he never used it, perhaps because it was cheaper to rely on Chinese labor, no matter what the cost to them. Never again were tunnel projects on that scale carried out by manual labor alone.

In June, 1867, the Chinese rebelled against low pay and long hours. They dropped their picks and shovels and brought work in Tunnel Number 6 to a dead stop. They demanded a $10 raise (to $40 a month) and a cut in the workday to ten hours in the open, or eight in the tunnels. What they wanted was fair and reasonable, but Crocker blamed the strike on "paid agitators" working secretly for his rival, the Union Pacific Railroad.

There was more behind the strike than wages and hours. The Chinese, wrote the Sacramento *Union*, were striking against "the right of the overseers of the company to either whip them or restrain them from leaving the road when they desired to seek other employment." Crocker was forcing people to work against their will, penning them up in detention camps, refusing them the right to change jobs, and using physical punishment to control them. Determined to do as he pleased, Crocker refused to compromise. He cut off shipments of the special food from China while the one-eyed Strobridge stomped about with a pick handle, threatening to beat up anyone who talked back. Crocker set a deadline for the men to return to work. If the men showed up, no punishment. If they didn't, they would be fined the cost of keeping their foremen and draft animals idle as long as the strike lasted.

What choice did they have? They were alone in a friendless land. They had no union to back them up, and public opinion was hostile. Few whites in California had any liking for the Chinese immigrants. Work—or starve, said the Central Pacific. The Chinese went back to their jobs.

When the last of the summit tunnels was completed, the railroad builders headed for the Nevada state line. It was the fall of 1867. The work crews were housed in old barns and sheds in the town of Truckee, California. A heavy snow came early, collapsing a barn and killing four men. The intense cold froze many workers to death. Before winter ended, the snowfall totaled 40 feet. Still, in the harshest weather, the builders graded the roadbed beyond the state line, into Nevada.

To shield the tracks and to keep the road clear

for work and traffic, snowsheds and galleries of enormous strength were constructed. They were a series of timber tunnels fixed to the sides of the mountains so that avalanches of snow and ice could pass over them easily. The figures give some idea of the immense size of the task of building them. The project used 65 million feet of timber and 900 tons of bolts and spikes. The total length of the sheds and galleries was 37 miles. The snowsheds built by the laborers stood the tests of winter superbly. Not one collapsed or was badly damaged.

The railroad kept moving on, down the east slope of the Sierra and out into the desert. From here on the workers would battle not snow and ice but sunbaked sand—500 miles of desert with only a few water holes all the way across Nevada into western Utah. Parts of the desert were so bad, said the jokesters, that "even the jackrabbits carried canteens and haversacks."

The problem of obtaining supplies added to the hardships. The desert offered no wood, no coal, no food, and almost no water. Everything had to be brought in over long distances and difficult terrain. Thousands of Chinese climbed into wagons and, with tools and provisions, rolled out upon the desert to prepare the grade for the track layers behind them. They began work at one spot in the morning, and by evening equipment, tents, bunks, and offices were ten miles away at another site. Overnight, towns of 5,000 inhabitants were created that by daybreak were deserted villages. A well-built roadbed stretched between morning and evening sites.

How the rails were laid is described by a historian of the Central Pacific:

Iron trains were scheduled so that the first one each day pulled in and was unloaded at sunrise, while the work force breakfasted and was marshaled for the day's planned stint. The empty iron train backed into the clear. . . . Small flatcars were loaded with ties, rails, fastenings, and drawn by horses out to the end of the track. Ties were put down. The iron gangs laid down the rails while a Chinese distributed spikes, two to each tie; another distributed fishplates; a third the bolts and nuts to fasten them. Two to each side of the track came the spikers, nailing rails to ties. Two more men followed to adjust and tighten the fishplates, the flatcar rolling ahead in the meantime, the next pair of rails clanking down. Emptied at last, the car was tipped off the track to make way for a loaded one. [The Chinese] fetched the seven more ties needed to bring each rail length up to standard specifications and inserted them in place. Other [Chinese] spiked them fast. The boss checked and trued the rails.

By late November, 1868, the railhead was nearing the Utah border. The outpost force of 3,000 Chinese preparing the roadbed "had wrought a near-miracle," wrote a historian long after. They had succeeded in building a grade through a chain of canyons so deep, so gloomy, and so cramped that it was said "no man or animal ever had traversed it before. This magnificent grading job, done under the most primitive conditions and in almost complete silence and obscurity, stands today as one of the great engineering feats. . . ."

With winter came brutal, paralyzing cold. The temperature in northeastern Nevada could drop to 50 degrees below zero. The earth froze rock hard. The Chinese had to resort to gunpowder to blast it open.

By the spring of 1869, Crocker's crews were pushing across the salt flats of northwest Utah, laying track at the fast pace of four miles a day. The end was near. The two lines, the Union Pacific and the Central Pacific, were racing to meet at Promontory Point, just above the Great Salt

Lake. The grading gangs—Irish workers heading west and Chinese workers heading east—drew close. The Irish, resenting the Chinese competition, decided to terrorize them. They secretly placed a charge of blasting powder so that it blew up Chinese workers, killing them. Strobridge protested, but the Union Pacific ignored him. The Irish did it again. This time the Chinese took their defense into their own hands. They planted a powder charge that killed several Irishmen and injured several more. That ended the undeclared war.

On May 10, 1869, the last tie was laid to complete the first transcontinental railroad. As the golden spike was rammed home, the news was telegraphed all over the country. The Irish and the Chinese were present at the ceremony at Promontory Point. But when the official photograph was taken, the Chinese were forgotten.

They Mined the Gold

華僑

THEY WERE LEFT out of the photograph, those Chinese railroad men, but they did not vanish from history. They went on spinning the steel web that tied modern America together. It's hard to name a railroad line in the West or South that the Chinese did not build in whole or in part. From way up in Alaska to deep down in Texas they moved by the thousands, making the roadbeds, digging the tunnels, and laying the tracks of the Southern Pacific, the Northern Pacific, the Canadian Pacific, the Oregon Central, the Seattle and Walla Walla, the Atlantic and Pacific, the California Central and California South, the Virginia and Truckee, the Eureka and Palisades, the Carson and Colorado, the Texas Pacific, the Houston and Texas Central, the Alabama and Chattanooga. . . .

It is estimated that about 1,200 Chinese—10 percent of the work force—died while building the Central Pacific, and the bones of uncounted others are buried beside the tracks of many other lines. But who remembered them? Only ten years after the celebration at Promontory Point, novelist Robert Louis Stevenson was traveling to California by train. He noticed a group of Chinese railroad men sitting segregated from the white passengers in a separate car. "Stupid ill-feeling," he wrote. The whites "seemed never to have looked at them, listened to them, or thought of them."

Building the railroads would have been achievement enough. But during those years the Chinese could be found doing many other kinds of work as well. Many of those who worked on the railroads had come out of California's gold mines.

In 1848, news of the discovery of flakes of yellow metal in a California river started a wild gold rush. A hundred thousand men infected by gold fever poured in from everywhere. Chinese people already in California wrote home of the Gold Rush, and the word spread. In the early 1850s, advertisements appeared in newspapers on the

Chinese coast to attract passengers for American ships making return trips from China. In 1851, drawn by the lure of riches, nearly 3,000 Chinese sailed for what they called the "Golden Mountain." The next year the number leaped to 20,000. Most of them came from one part of southeastern China, Kwangtung Province.

San Francisco was the starting point for the Chinese treasure hunters. As soon as they landed, they bought supplies and set off for the gold districts. Observers noted their strange appearance:

Crowds of Chinamen were bound for the diggings, each man with a bamboo laid across his shoulder, from both ends of which was suspended a higgledy-piggledy collection of mining tools, Chinese baskets and boxes, immense boots and a variety of Chinese "fixins" which no one but a Chinaman could tell the use of. . . .

Another wrote:

They are mostly dressed in the national costume, petticoat trousers reaching to the knees, big jackets, lined and quilted, and huge basket hats made of split bamboo. The lower part of their legs are encased in blue cotton stockings made of cloth and with soles fully an inch in depth.

The goldfields were scattered in a belt of hills spanning 150 miles north to south. For two years before the Chinese arrived, gold seekers had been sweeping over the Sierra foothills. Few of them knew anything about mining. Skimming the surface gold was easy, and overnight some men found fortunes in dry gulches and ravines. When that gold was gone, harder and more skilled methods were needed to extract the metal from the wet diggings of rivers and creeks.

The early Chinese miners worked with a device called a cradle. It was an oblong box mounted on rockers. The miners shoveled dirt into a hopper at one end, poured in water, then rocked the cradle violently until the sand washed away and the heavier gold was caught by cleats along the bottom of the box.

The Chinese soon introduced an improved method of mining that astonished the whites, who simply panned the gold dust from the rivers. With a water wheel and a mechanized system of bailing buckets on rope pulleys, the Chinese drained stretches of river to get at the gold on the bottom. Thus, they were able to find gold that earlier adventurers had missed. The Chinese miners' success at working claims others had given up roused the white miners to jealousy and hatred.

Panning for California gold in 1852. (CALIFORNIA HISTORICAL SOCIETY)

At first, the Chinese had been looked upon by the whites as people interestingly different from themselves. But as more and more Chinese came into the mining districts—and made their ingenuity pay off—the tolerance gave way to anger. "Three years ago," said the Shasta *Courier* in 1853, "it was a matter of no little curiousity to the American miner to see a real live representative of the Celestial Empire, with his wooden shoes, his prodigious hat of fantastical proportions, his shaven head, his long black queue dangling at his feet. . . . But the time has now arrived when the Chinaman begins to be regarded with feelings other than those of mere idle curiousity."

White miners held mass meetings and resolved to get rid of this competition. In district after district the Chinese were denied the right to mine, and they were forced out by acts of violence. The California legislature passed a $3 monthly license tax on foreign miners. The tax kept going higher and higher, making many Chinese quit mining or go to work for others. The tax was aimed at other foreigners as well, but it was principally enforced against the Chinese. "The gold mines were preserved by nature for Americans only," wrote one newspaper. "We will share

A mining camp of Chinese in California, 1851. (WELLS FARGO BANK
HISTORY ROOM)

our interest in gold mines with none but American citizens."

When hard-rock, or deep, mining began, businessmen took over from the lone prospector. It took capital to tap gold deposits deep beneath the ground. This kind of mining meant sinking shafts and driving tunnels and blasting rock and crushing quartz to extract the gold. Many Chinese hired themselves out to white mine operators. As day laborers, they got about half the pay of white men.

The skill of the Chinese surprised the mine owners. "They surpass the white man in the same mine," reported one owner. Shamefully, such compliments didn't bring a raise in pay, but the loss of jobs. White workers pressed mine operators to fire the Chinese.

Instead of working for whites, some of the immigrant miners hired themselves out to newly formed Chinese companies set up by prosperous merchants. These men bought up old claims and set crews of 15 to 20 miners to working them. The crew foreman supplied food and tools, and took all the gold for the company. The miners were paid in wages.

Men from the same villages or clans in China usually preferred to live and work together in

California. "Chinatowns" sprang up to serve their and the white miners' needs. The Chinese started laundries and opened restaurants, boardinghouses, and general stores. Some Chinatowns in the mining regions grew as large as several thousand people.

The lure of new diggings soon drew miners beyond the borders of California. Surely there must be gold hidden in other crevices of that vast West, they thought. When news came of a gold strike, a flood of prospectors poured in that direction, thousands of Chinese among them. They tried their luck in Nevada, Colorado, Montana, Idaho, Oregon, and Washington. The most adventurous headed for the goldfields along the Fraser and Columbia rivers in Canada. Everywhere, long after the white miners had drifted away, the Chinese continued to extract the last ounces of gold dust.

In 1870, the Chinese formed the largest single ethnic group of miners in the West—17,000 people. One out of every four miners was a man from China—a fact few people know.

They Farmed the Land and Fished the Sea
華僑

TODAY THE WORLD knows the great valley of California as a fabled food basket. But the earth those fruits and vegetables grow in wasn't worth much until the Chinese reclaimed it.

Further back than history can remember, big chunks of land in the Sacramento and San Joaquin river valleys were nothing but swamp. Tule land, it was called; the term was taken from an Indian word that means a kind of bulrush that grows in marshy land. The huge delta of the two rivers was made up of mucky deposits formed by river-borne sediment and the decayed remains of grasses and reeds.

In the 1850s, farmers knew there was rich soil in those swamps. But how could they get in and work a swamp? It would take hard labor, and lots of it. Big California was small in population, and white workers shunned such backbreaking labor.

As the Chinese immigrants stepped ashore, American farmers hired some of them to build levees in the delta. Then, as many Chinese left the goldfields, the farmers hired more for the task of draining the marshlands. Companies that were set up to do large-scale land reclamation used roughly the same work-gang system as the railroads. They signed on Chinese foremen, giving them contracts to build a levee at a fixed rate. The foremen hired their countrymen, put up tents, took care of supplies and food, and paid each worker $1 a day.

With pick and shovel the Chinese built miles and miles of levees, ditches, and dikes. They reclaimed thousands of acres of land so that farmers could grow abundant crops. Land worth $1 or $2 an acre before reclamation was worth $20 to $100 an acre afterward.

In building the railroads and reclaiming the tule lands, the Chinese gave California a huge economic boost. One expert worked it out in dollars and cents. He told a U.S. Senate committee that the Chinese had increased the value of property in the state by $300 million. That is a lot of money today; over 100 years ago, it meant even more.

With the valley lands ready for growing crops,

the farmers needed laborers to plant, cultivate, and harvest. Again, they turned to the Chinese. Machinery could handle much of the work on a wheat ranch. But hand labor was needed for the intensive, specialized fruit and vegetable crops. And good profits demanded a cheap and plentiful labor supply. The growers had that readily available, in the Chinese—a despised and powerless minority. The Chinese were denied any work a white person might want to do. Their human right to exist was hardly recognized. For the growers, it was the perfect setup. They could hire Chinese workers at wages even below the subsistence level.

The growers were getting a double bargain. The Chinese were not only forced to work for next to nothing—they proved to be extremely capable. "They are the mainstay of the orchardist," said the *Pacific Rural Press,* "the only supply of labor he can depend upon. They are expert pickers and packers of fruit. It is difficult to see how our annual fruit crop could be harvested and prepared for market without the Chinaman."

A fact the growers did not care to make known was that the Chinese knew more than they did about agriculture. Most of the growers were new to farming. The Chinese "actually taught their

overlords how to plant, cultivate, and harvest or-
chard and garden crops," wrote Carey McWilliams, a historian who has studied California agriculture. It was a skill the Chinese did not pick up
overnight in America. They came from a land
where intensive cultivation was an ancient tradition.

America owes a great deal to China's agriculture—not only for the best varieties of oranges we
enjoy, but for many other fruits and vegetables
grown commercially in the United States. The
soybean (whose multiple food and industrial values we at last appreciate) can be traced back to
China 3,000 years before Christ. Wheat, millet,
and barley were grown in China many centuries
before Europeans learned of them. All of our ce-
reals but maize, sorghum, and some forms of oats
originated in Asia. The common fruit trees of the
temperate zone, except for the pecan and the per-
simmon, came from Asia, too. So did most citrus
fruits. And animals? Horses, donkeys, cattle,
sheep, goats, hogs, and chickens all came from
Asia.

By the 1870s, three out of four farm workers in
California were Chinese. In the vineyards they
harvested the grapes, and they dug the under-

ground wine cellars. They picked apples, peaches, pears, cherries, olives, citrus fruits, and cotton. They grew pumpkins, celery, asparagus, and cabbages. They built the roads, stone bridges, rock walls, and irrigation ditches that added permanently to the value of the land. All along the Pacific Coast the Chinese harvested hops and strawberries, crops that required painful stooping or squatting. As machinery moved into agriculture, it left the least desirable tasks to be done by hand. To weed sugar beets, for instance, the Chinese had to work on their hands and knees, leaving a bloody trail on the ground.

Thousands spent their bleak lives keeping on the move from season to season and place to place, taking work of any kind to survive. A man might be picking fruit around Watsonville, California, in the summer, cutting sardines in Monterey, California, in November, packing salmon in the Alaska canneries in the wintertime. Then it would be back to California to harvest the asparagus in the spring. It was a dreary, grinding routine that barely kept body and soul together. Until 1900 the Chinese moved up and down the valleys by the season, just as other Asians and the Mexicans would do after them.

The wages were always low. In Napa County,

California, in the 1870s, a Chinese migrant worker would get $1 for picking 1,500 pounds of grapes in a day. A dollar a day seemed the grower's magic number, no matter what the quantity or quality of the labor, or the cost of living. The Chinese did not take low wages quietly. They went on strike many times, demanding pay at least equal to what whites were getting. But the protests rarely succeeded. The growers could always turn the acid stream of anti-Chinese feeling against the workers.

Some Chinese managed to save a bit from their low pay, rent small plots of land, and become tenant farmers. They would pay the landlord a half or a third of their crops. The Chinese tenant farmers usually raised strawberries, peanuts, or vegetables.

As truck gardeners, the Chinese were rated the best. They worked plots on the edges of towns and sold their vegetables from wagons, driving up and down the city streets. When he visited San Francisco in the 1870s, Polish novelist Henryk Sienkiewicz was impressed by the truck gardens he saw:

San Francisco is situated on arid dunes and sandy hills, and yet whoever goes to the outskirts of the city will

A grocery store in San Francisco's Chinatown, 1892. (NEW YORK
PUBLIC LIBRARY PICTURE COLLECTION)

perceive at the ends of unfinished streets, on the hills, valleys, and slopes, on the roadsides, in fact, everywhere, small vegetable gardens encircling the city with one belt of greenness. The ant-like labor of the Chinese has transformed the sterile sands into the most fertile black earth. . . . The fruits and vegetables, raspberries and strawberries under the care of Chinese gardeners grow to a fabulous size. I have seen strawberries as large as small pears and heads of cabbage four times the size of European heads, and pumpkins the size of our wash tubs. . . .

On the peninsula south of San Francisco, the Chinese started a flower-growing industry. During the 1890s they began raising sweet peas and asters, bringing the mixed cut flowers in to the city for sale. When the Japanese introduced chrysanthemums, the Chinese grew them, too.

Fishing was another way of making a living. Native Americans had always fished the rivers and seas, but the white frontiersmen did not at first do so. The whites preferred beans and beef to the fish and vegetables that were ancient Chinese pleasures. So, the Chinese created a fishing industry in the West. Their boats, built like traditional sampans and junks, and their fine mesh nets brought from Kwangtung were well suited to the work.

The Chinese fishermen settled in villages along the shore. One of the villages, on the south side of Rincon Point, San Francisco, housed 150 people. A reporter visited it in 1854.

They have 25 boats, some of which may be seen at all hours moving over the waters—some going to, others returning from the fishing-grounds. The houses are placed in a line on each side of the one street of the village, and look neat and comfortable. Here and there, a group is seen making fishlines, and with their crude machines stacking in heaps the quantities of fish which, lying on all sides around, dry in the sun, and emit an ancient and fishlike odor. The fish which they catch consist of sturgeon, rates, and shark, and large quantities of herring. The latter are dried whole, while the larger are cut into thin pieces. When they are sufficiently dry, they are packed in barrels, boxes or sacks, and sent into town to be disposed of to those of their countrymen who are going to the mines or are bound upon long voyages. . . . The average yield of their fishing a day was about 3,000 pounds, and they found ready sale for them.

For many years the expert Chinese led the way

in fishing the coastal waters from Tacoma, Washington, to San Diego, California. They ran all the shrimp camps on San Francisco Bay, and on the Columbia River they manned the salmon canneries. Even the taste for shellfish delicacies—crab, lobster, shrimp, abalone—whites owe to the Chinese who introduced them in the West.

In the mid-1800s the factories of California were small local operations set up to meet Pacific Coast needs. In 1870, about half the 5,000 workers employed in them were Chinese. Most of the Chinese were in the cigar industry. The others were scattered among the boot and shoe industry and the woolens and garment trades.

A greater number of Chinese were working as domestic servants, laundrymen, or restauranteurs than as industrial workers. But not because they preferred such occupations. It was racial prejudice that kept the Chinese out of the better jobs whites wanted for themselves. Racism left open only a very few kinds of work in which the Chinese might not be the victims of competition and discrimination.

There were few women in the frontier West to do the tasks commonly restricted to them—cooking, cleaning, washing, ironing, and serving.

With better jobs denied them, many Chinese immigrants opened laundries, a business that they could run for themselves. (LIBRARY OF CONGRESS)

With the shortage of women workers, whites who could afford servants hired the Chinese. In the 1870s there were some 5,000 Chinese employed as house servants in San Francisco. Their work was useful. But it was of small economic importance to the community compared with what many more thousands of Chinese did in the mines and on the railroads and farms.

Either driven out of other work or preferring not to face racism, the Chinese opened laundries in the West and elsewhere. Unfortunately, the laundryman quickly became the average American's image of a Chinese person. So, too, with the Chinese restaurant owner and his Chinese waiters. Again, this was a trade a man could run for himself, and one where he served his own countrymen within the Chinatowns that were growing up in America. Only a small investment was needed to open a laundry or a restaurant. This was an important consideration, for few Chinese had the money, or could borrow the capital, to launch bigger enterprises. The risk was small and the labor was their own and their families'.

Where They Came From

華僑

WHEN THE CHINESE arrived on California's shore, what did the Americans know about them?

Most of us know too little of our own country's story, and we know less of any other's. About Asia, so remote and so different, we know probably the least. Two hundred years ago, when the first connection was made between the new United States and the old China, few Americans even knew where China was.

Yet in the 1780s at least 100 pioneers from China were already settled on the Pacific Coast of Canada. They had come from Kwangtung Province on an English ship to build a fort and a frontier village on Vancouver Island. Among them were seamen and pilots, architects and engineers, coopers and carpenters. They were a "hardy, industrious, and vigorous" people, the English sea captain said, and they had sailed every part of the China Sea. Many of them stayed in America. They explored the Northwest Coast 20 years before the Lewis and Clark expedition "discovered" the Pacific region.

The Chinese had proved their seafaring spirit and adventurous courage a long time before. In the sixteenth century, Chinese pioneers sailed for Mexico and Peru in Spanish galleons built in Manila by Chinese craftsmen. By the time the American nation was born, the Chinese were familiar with North and South America from Canada down to Peru. The Chinese left few records of their explorations, for the simple reason that they were forbidden by law to leave their country. Since they went illegally, they risked beheading if they talked or wrote about their voyages.

Much later, the Chinese again formed a link with America. The Boston Tea Party is a favorite story in the history books. But how many know that the tea was not English—it was Chinese? The English loved the teas their ships brought from China so much that the high cost almost bankrupted England. To get some of that money back, the English ordered the American colonies to pay a high tax on Chinese tea brought in via England. When the angry colonists dumped the Chinese tea into Boston Harbor, it signaled the beginning of the American Revolution.

While America was still a colony, she was not allowed to trade directly with China. That was England's privilege. In these years, England truly ruled the seas.

Later, England forced China to open her ports to the opium trade. England stood to make much money from this. The poppies from which the opium came were grown in India, and the drug was manufactured by a British company with royal approval. The opium was then shipped to China, against Chinese law, and sold at an enormous profit. The Chinese had been using a milder form of opium for centuries. The Indian opium was so powerful that smoking it was addictive.

The Chinese government did not want the opium sold in China because of the terrible harm it did. Yet the English, concerned only with profits, forced it upon China through military power. The income from opium, they callously decided, would make up for England's trade losses. (England's economic problem was due partly to the cost of her many wars—and partly to her passion for tea.)

When the outraged Chinese dumped millions of dollars' worth of opium into the Pearl River at

Canton, a British naval force invaded China. The Chinese resisted, but lost the Opium Wars.

The first Yankee ship to reach the Orient was the *Empress of China*. She arrived at Canton in 1784, bringing a cargo of ginseng root, a medicinal herb grown by the Iroquois tribes but so common in China that no one there needed it. It was but one sign of Americans' ignorance about China. George Washington, who had never met any Chinese, thought they were "white." (Apparently he hadn't read about them, either.) Even brilliant men like Benjamin Franklin, Thomas Jefferson, and John Adams knew nothing about China.

The Yankee traders knew even less. They saw China as a strange and mysterious place.

They might have learned something about China from the Chinese pioneers on America's West Coast. But virtually no one knew they were there. And what if their presence had been known? Historian Stan Steiner points out:

[*The Americans*] *probably would not have recognized them as pioneers. They did not behave as pioneers should, for they made no attempt to possess the land they explored, and the emperors of China did not send their navy, the largest in the Pacific, to invade America.*

Pioneers on the frontier came to conquer. The ethic

A busy street in Canton, the port city of Kwangtung Province in southeast China from which most Chinese emigrated to the United States. (NEW YORK PUBLIC LIBRARY PICTURE COLLECTION)

and the ideal of the pioneering Europeans was to remake America in their own image. . . . The Chinese had come with a different mind. For to possess and conquer the land was a foreign idea to them. Here and elsewhere they came to savor the adventure, to explore with curiosity, and to become wealthy. It was not their need to remake America into an image of China; the thought was absurd.

Americans learned nothing about China until traders, missionaries, and diplomats began to send home their impressions of the country.

The American traders held great hopes for profit in China. By 1790, all the Atlantic seaports from Salem, Massachusetts, to Newport, Rhode Island, were sending ships to China. Though some men grew rich, the rewards of trade never matched their hopes. Disappointed in business, the traders had few good things to say about the Chinese.

A study of the records left by scores of American traders who journeyed to China before 1840 shows how little respect they had for the Chinese and their culture. They called the Chinese superstitious, dishonest, and cruel. They said the government officials they dealt with were deceitful and corrupt. And they looked down on the people

A scene on the Pearl River in Canton in the 1850s. (NEW YORK
PUBLIC LIBRARY PICTURE COLLECTION)

for lacking the courage to do something about the oppressive conditions under which they lived. These impressions of China circulated widely in America through reports, letters, gossip, newspaper stories, and books.

Diplomats representing their governments in China—most of them European—wrote books that said most of the same things. One Englishman compared the empire of China to an old battleship that was kept afloat by her officers way past the time when she should have sunk. The reports of the Christian missionaries in China were not much different, either. The missionaries had small success in winning converts in what they considered to be a pagan nation. They added to the distorted picture that most people had with angry moralistic attacks upon the vices they saw—gambling, prostitution, and drug use.

The accounts of most travelers were full of astonishment at the "very peculiar" tastes and habits of the Chinese. To think that they made medicine of the horn of a rhinoceros! Or soup from a bird's nest! That they ate all manner of strange and disgusting things! Chinese theater and music seemed "weird" and "detestable." Westerners also poked fun at the Chinese way of doing things "backward"—imagine wearing white for mourning, buying a coffin while still alive, dressing women in pants and men in gowns, writing up and down the page instead of across from left to right, eating sweets first and soups last. . . .

Westerners looked at China with blinders on. They were unable to understand the Chinese as they really were. Everything was measured with a European or American yardstick. It was the rare traveler who tried to judge the Chinese by their own standards and tastes.

So even before the Chinese came to California by the thousands in the 1850s, they were the victims of racism. Fear and suspicion were lying in wait for the Chinese immigrants. Without giving the Chinese a chance to show who and what they were, the American majority had made up its collective mind. The Chinese were seen as different in color and different in culture. And because they were different, they were held to be inferior.

Of course the Chinese were different. But how? And was it anything to be afraid of? Or to ridicule?

China is a big country, second in land area only to the Soviet Union. It covers over four million square miles. Much of this territory is frontier, not thickly populated. The Chinese heartland is made up of 18 provinces. China is divided into two major regions, the North and the South, just as the United States is.

North China is a brown and dusty plain, thoroughly cultivated by hand. Irrigation water from the Yellow River and its tributaries is used for farming. The soil is highly productive (the main crops are wheat and millet), but the area produces much less than the American corn and wheat belts. And heavy floods breaking the dikes have again and again caused terrible destruction and loss of life.

South China has a milder climate, and abundant rainfall. The Yangtze River, when it reaches the central plain, flows through a lush green region where flowers and fruits of every sort grow, and conditions for the cultivation of rice are superb. Rice has been the backbone of Chinese life. It needs intensive cultivation; two or even three harvests are produced from one field every year. The water buffalo is the work animal, and the waterways are the main highways. People travel and transport goods via small sampan or large junk.

Heartland China is a checkerboard of small to medium-sized valleys. It is not a vast stretch of unbroken farmland like the American Midwest. Despite the need to feed a huge, growing population, no more than one-fourth of China's land is under regular cultivation.

The populated area of China is only about half as large as the populated area of the United States. Yet China has to feed about four times as many people. It has always taken unceasing human labor in both North and South to extract from nature food enough for survival. And such effort may be brought to nothing by the frequent natural disasters: drought, flood, pestilence, famine.

Although all Chinese are of Mongoloid racial stock, the Chinese are quite varied in appearance. No Chinese person's skin is truly yellow. Skin tones shade from a sallow off-white to bronze and olive hues. The so-called Mongoloid type is made up of many different strains. Chinese may be flat-nosed or hawk-nosed; most have black hair, but some are redheaded; some men grow beards and others do not; and the North Chinese are commonly taller than the South Chinese. Even what Westerners think of as the slanted eye—really a fold of skin over the eye—is by no means universal.

In culture, too, there are differences among the Chinese. The majority of the Chinese are Han people; they take their name from an admired early dynasty. These people are the developers and carriers of what is commonly considered the traditional Chinese civilization. The many non-Han people include the Manchus in the northeast; the Mongols of Inner Mongolia; the Moslems in the west and Sinkiang; the Tibetans; and many tribal peoples of the hill country in the south and southwest.

The Moslems are different in religion, of course. But the main difference between the Han people and the minorities is that the traditional languages of the minority groups are not Chinese.

The Han people use variants of Chinese that are as different from one another as German is from Italian. A man from Canton, in the south, cannot understand or make himself understood by a man from Peking, in the north. The regional variations in speech are so great that some language experts consider Chinese to be not one tongue, but a family of tongues.

The language spoken by the majority of Chinese is known to Westerners as Mandarin. The Chinese call it *kuo-yü*, "the national speech." Modern Chinese governments have promoted it as the standard speech in an attempt to make nationwide communication easier.

The written language is not spelled out in the letters of an alphabet, but in characters of beautiful pictorial quality. Each symbol, distinct and recognizable, has a meaning that is separate from any sound; it exists as a picture.

It is not easy to learn to read and write Chinese characters. The largest dictionary has over 40,000 characters in it, but one can be literate with a knowledge of 3,000 of them.

For 3,000 years, only 5 or 10 percent of the males could read or write. Until recently, women were not taught to read and write. Under the educational system of the People's Republic of China, the literacy rate has risen considerably.

The Chinese writing system adapts to the variety of dialects. Chinese who might not understand each other can, if they are literate, communicate in writing. The Chinese characters are like Arabic numerals (1, 2, 3, 4, etc.), which are understood everywhere even though they are pronounced differently in different languages.

Written English has changed more in a brief time than Chinese has over a much longer period. The Chinese today can read works written 3,000 or 4,000 years ago. English-speaking people have trouble reading the works of Chaucer, written less than 600 years ago. The continuity of the written language has given the Chinese a powerful feeling for their past, and has bound them closely together as their civilization has developed.

Today the Chinese people constitute one-fifth to one-quarter of all mankind. There are no exact figures available, but the best estimate of China's population is one billion. In 1600, it was 200 million. In the 1850s, when Chinese immigrants began coming to California, it had doubled to 400 million. The increase seems enormous. But China is much bigger than Europe and in roughly the same 250-year period, Europe's population rose from 100 million to 650 million, multiplying more than six times, rather than just twice.

Unlike Europe, which is divided into many nations, the subcontinent of China has remained a single country. China is the oldest continuously self-governing nation in the world. It has been held together by a way of life that stretches back thousands of years. From ancient times until the Communist revolution succeeded in 1949, there were two basic classes: the peasants, who lived in the villages, and the people of property, who lived in the towns and cities. The upper class was made up of landlords, merchants, scholars, and officials.

The peasant class—the farmers—were far more numerous; four out of five Chinese have always lived on and worked the land. But the upper class in the cities ruled the people of the countryside. The few controlled the lives of the many.

For 3,000 years, poverty was the accepted lot of the farmers. Most of their meager income went for food, the tiny remainder for rent, light, heat, and clothing. Until very recently that wretched existence kept life expectancy at only 26 years. The bedrock of Chinese society has been the peasant village, with the family—not the individual—the key to survival and the center of authority.

The reverence for parents instilled by family life was carried over into loyalty to the rulers of the nation and obedience to the government. Great respect was paid to the elders. The father was supreme. He controlled the use of all family property and income. When he died, the oldest son became head of the family. The father's voice was decisive in arranging the marriages of his children. The parents were held responsible for their children.

Just as age dominated youth in the Chinese family, so did male dominate female. A girl's marriage was arranged; it was not for love. And the bride came under the rule of her mother-in-law.

Women had no economic independence. In the past, peasant women were all illiterate and only a small number of upper-class women learned to read and write.

The inferior position of women was only one sign of the Chinese social system of higher and lower status. The wife was bound to her husband, the son to his father, and the people to their ruler. Within the family, and in the broad world outside, the central fact of life was the division between the ruler and the ruled. And if a husband, father, or ruler acted like a tyrant, law and custom did little to change that.

Chinese raised in the traditional manner knew automatically where they stood in the family and in society. There was a certain secure feeling in knowing that if you did the part allotted to you, you could expect others to do the parts allotted to them.

When a Chinese father died, his land was equally divided among his sons. By constant divisions of the land, parcels were kept small and peasant families were kept poor. Disease and famine, added to the scarcity of land, set limits to family size. The average peasant family consisted of five persons—father, mother, two children, and a grandparent. They lived in small villages of per-haps 75 households; the villages were clustered around a market town. About 18 villages sur-rounded such a town, and none of them was more than a few miles from the town center. The round trip to market could easily be made in a day on foot, by donkey, or in a sampan.

The average market community of villages added up to perhaps 1,500 households and 7,500 people. In this small sphere the people conducted their economic and social lives. Here they cele-brated their festivals, met in their secret society lodges, and paid their rent and taxes. Each com-munity was largely self-sufficient.

Family and village relationships were the most important aspects of Chinese life. Often whole villages were inhabited by a single family line or clan, especially in the provinces of Kwangtung and Fukien, from which most emigrants to Amer-ica have come. The Hung family, for instance, settled in Yinglin Township in Fukien Province in about the year 1000. By the 1950s, the Hung clan had grown so large that it occupied 57 towns and villages of various sizes in the area. Next door in Kwangtung Province, four of every five peasants lived with their clans, usually one clan to a village. Even when there were several clans in a village, each one usually lived in its own neighborhood.

Each family community was a society run by its own rules. In the villages, the local headmen were the unofficial government. The imperial government depended on the headmen to settle disputes and to ensure the collection of taxes. If the more powerful clans exploited the weaker ones, the weaker clans might band together, claiming to have discovered a common ancestor, or they might simply form an alliance to resist the oppressors. Ancient clan feelings and disputes could lead to violence, and villages sometimes warred against each other. It might take government troops to stop the fighting.

Whenever the Chinese left their homeland to try their luck overseas, they naturally carried with them the way of life learned in their clans and villages.

The ideas people hold and the way they live influence each other. The Chinese for countless generations have had to struggle with the forces of nature to survive. Their art and religion reflect the awe in which they hold nature. And living close together in their villages has made them a highly social people. Their experiences have molded a view of human existence and of society different from that held by more industrialized peoples.

The meaning of life and ideas about how it should be lived have been expressed for the Chinese in the thoughts and writings of Confucius. He was an aristocrat who lived some 2,500 years ago. He taught moral behavior and urged people to try to live in harmony with the unseen forces of nature. According to Confucius, the achievement of a peaceful life in harmony with the universe is best done by serving parents with filial love. Maintain the universal harmony of man and nature, he said, by doing the right thing at the right time.

Confucius's thoughts influenced both family life and the conduct of government. Confucius was not concerned with the afterlife or the supernatural; his central interest was in man's present place in the real world. He taught that a ruler must behave morally to earn his authority and power.

In the Chinese state, authority was centered in the man at the top—the emperor. The emperor's ministers and the government officials below them exercised his authority. A system of appointed and salaried officials who were trained in schools and had to pass written examinations grew up over the centuries. China led the world in developing government by trained administrators and officials.

The Confucian way was modified down through the many dynasties of Chinese history. For over half of the last 1,000 years, alien invaders ruled China. Inevitably, there was conflict and change, but the strong pattern of traditional culture remained.

Who They Were

華僑

PEOPLE BY THE hundreds, thousands, and millions have migrated from their homelands to some other part of the world. During the 1800s, the whole continent of Europe was on the move. In a span of 100 years, 40 million Europeans came to the New World. It was the largest movement of peoples in world history. The Europeans all went westward, and for the same reasons. They wanted to escape poverty, to gain liberty, or to be free to worship as they pleased.

The Chinese, too, have contributed chapters to the story of human migration. In the seventh century Chinese adventurers went to islands not far from the mainland. About 700 years later, a second wave of emigrants went as far as Africa, with some Chinese settling in the East Indies and the Philippines. Another wave of emigrants left China in the mid-1800s, around the time of the great European migration. The number of Chinese who sailed abroad was not great, especially when measured against China's large population. Still, by 1930 there were eight million Chinese settled around the world.

Most of the Chinese emigrants came from just one province—Kwangtung. Why only from that part of China? And why did they leave home? When people pick up and go, it's usually because there is a push and a pull. Something at home drives them to leave, and something abroad attracts them.

If you look at a map of China, you'll note that Kwangtung is on the southeastern coast. At the heart of the province is the port city of Canton. Most Chinese who crossed the seas came from the counties around Canton. Two of these counties, Chungshan and Toishan, are sea-washed peninsulas below the mouth of the Pearl River. Pioneers from this region had for centuries explored unknown lands abroad. Their mastery of seamanship and of the craft of shipbuilding was legendary.

The peasants of Kwangtung were also known for their spirit of independence. Both geography and climate forced them to be self-reliant. They had always resisted assimilation by northern invaders, and they clung to the language and cus-

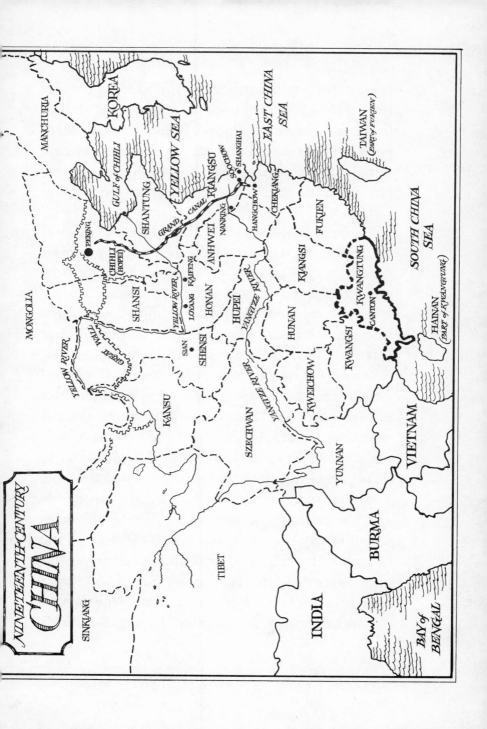

toms of their tribal ancestors. In the Mongol invasion of the 1200s, the people of Kwangtung put up fierce and heroic resistance. When the alien Manchus overran China and set up the last imperial dynasty (1644–1912), the Kwangtung peasants struggled the hardest against despotic rule by invaders.

A third invasion, this time by the English launching the Opium Wars, was met by a mass rebellion. The people of Kwangtung fought furiously to drive the English soldiers out, and they nearly succeeded. With defeat, however, China lost many rights. For example, Chinese goods leaving China were taxed, while foreign goods entering China came in duty free. A weakened China signed treaties that let other countries act as rulers over chunks of Chinese territory. For the first time, foreigners were allowed to make permanent homes in five port cities from Canton to Shanghai. These ports were also opened to trade.

The wars left China with a ruined countryside and the peasants with a heavy burden of taxes levied to pay the costs. The harsh methods of the tax collectors increased discontent and misery. By offering bribes, the rich, powerful people were able to avoid taxation. Population growth was outrunning food production. Living standards dropped lower and lower. The weaker clans fought with the stronger ones over land and water rights. Corrupt and lazy government officials made conditions still worse. Great numbers of poor people, without land or work, became desperate. The secret societies that had been formed to resist the alien rule of the Manchus grew in strength. Finally, in 1850, south China exploded in the so-called Taiping Rebellion. Its leader, born in a poor peasant village of Kwangtung, held forth the promise of rural reforms and the vision of equality for all. Fighting spread to many provinces. Hundreds of towns and cities were devastated in the revolutionary years of 1850–64, and perhaps 20 million people lost their lives. The revolution did not succeed, but the old system of empire was badly shaken.

So the emigration movement rose in a time of great troubles. War, famine, and poverty were the forces driving the peasants of Kwangtung and the city people of Canton from home. The prospect of high wages in the gold mines of California was all that was needed to lure them to America from their hard-hit homes.

Knowing something of their history, we can see that these emigrants were certainly not the

The interior of the North Fort, Peiho, in China, around 1860. China's emigration movement rose during a period of famine, poverty, and war. (NEW YORK PUBLIC LIBRARY PICTURE COLLECTION)

servile "coolies" many people thought them to be. The truth is, they were the tough and pugnacious sons of farmers and seafarers, a people raised in the most progressive province of China.

What the word "coolie" comes from is uncertain. The term usually means a cheap, unskilled laborer from the Orient. A contract labor system using coolies had developed in Southeast Asia, the West Indies, and Latin America in the early nineteenth century. After Britain abolished slavery in her colonies, plantation owners were looking for field labor they could control. They got British merchants in Hong Kong to procure Chinese laborers for them. The merchants in turn paid Chinese brokers to deliver the victims.

The men trapped by the brokers were often gamblers so deep in debt they had to offer their labor as payment. Some were prisoners captured in clan warfare, or men kidnapped off the streets —"shanghaied"—into semi-slavery. The coolie trade across the Pacific, like the African slave trade, was an evil thing. A high proportion of the coolies, held against their will belowdecks, died aboard ship because of terrible conditions. Those who reached their destinations were treated much like slaves.

Americans had heard of the coolie trade in

other countries. They mistakenly thought the Chinese immigrants to California were coolies, too. They feared that a kind of Chinese slavery might be starting on the West Coast. But the Chinese came of their own free will. (Though China forbade emigration, by this time the law was no longer enforced.) They were much like the Irish immigrants, uprooted from home by hard times and hunger.

What made it a bit easier to decide to go was word that Chinese merchants had already pioneered a settlement in California. A small number of merchants, knowing that the gold miners would need all kinds of supplies, had sailed promptly to San Francisco at the time of the Gold Rush and set up shop. They sold the miners grain, sugar, tea, rice, dried fruits, and spices, as well as tools, utensils, and clothing. The merchants were gentlemen who had no desire to dig gold. With them had come some craftsmen whose skills were helpful to the miners. They built the portable houses carried by wagon to the new mining towns. Some of those houses were early prefabs, brought in pieces from China and assembled in the goldfields.

There were only a few hundred Chinese immigrants in California in 1850. Within two years, the number swelled to over 20,000. It cost $40 to make the Pacific crossing. Since none but the merchants had passage money, a credit-ticket system was devised. Chinese merchants chartered space for groups of immigrants on ships that were making the crossing with passengers and cargo. The merchants then advanced ticket money to people who wanted to emigrate. They charged them high interest on top of the ticket price. When the immigrants arrived in San Francisco, they registered with a company representing the merchant. The company saw to it that the newcomers paid their debts in monthly installments.

About 300,000 Chinese made the Pacific crossing in the 30-year period starting with the Gold Rush. Almost all went into debt for their tickets. The ships carrying them were American or British. The fastest sailing vessels, called clippers, could cover the 7,000 miles from Canton to San Francisco in about 30 days. But most sailing ships took almost twice as long. When steamships entered the China trade in the mid-1860s, they crossed the Pacific in about 30 days.

A glimpse of the conditions aboard ship is offered by an Englishman. He made the voyage from China to California on the *Bald Eagle,* an American clipper carrying Chinese immigrants.

He sailed with the first-class passengers, but watched how the Chinese were treated. There were 400 aboard. Most were not allowed up on deck; only their cooks came up to prepare the meals. The Chinese ticket broker who had chartered the space had arranged for cooking places, bunks, and provisions. The pork and rice turned bad, and the bunks often broke down. When the weather got rough, cooking on deck was impossible, and the emigrants went without food.

Watching a ship arrive in San Francisco, a reporter said the main deck was packed solid with Chinese immigrants who were "gazing in silent wonder at the new land whose fame had reached them beyond the seas, and whose riches [they] have come to develop."

After the customs officers had cleared them, the immigrants crowded at the forward gangway. The reporter saw them leave ship:

A living stream of the blue-coated men of Asia, bending long bamboo poles across their shoulders, from which depend packages of bedding, matting, clothing, and things of which we know neither the names or the uses, pours down the plank the moment that the word is given, "All ready!"

They appear to be of an average age of 25 years—very

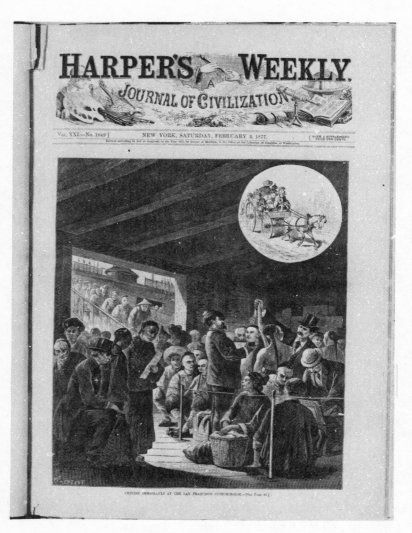

The arrival of Chinese immigrants at the San Francisco customs house was featured on page one in Harper's Weekly, February 3, 1877. *Note that the immigrants are mostly men.* (LIBRARY OF CONGRESS)

*few being under 15, and none apparently over 40 years
—and, though somewhat less in stature than Cauca-
sians, healthy, active, and able-bodied to a man. As they
come down onto the wharf, they separate into messes or
gangs of 10, 20, or 30 each, and being recognized through
some . . . incomprehensible . . . system of signs by agents
of the Six Companies [a Chinese organization] are assigned places on the wharf.*

*Each man carries his entire earthly possessions, and
few are overloaded. They are all dressed in coarse but
clean and new cotton blouses and loose baggy breeches,
blue cotton cloth stockings which reach to the knees, and
slippers or shoes with heavy wooden soles. . . . Most of
them carry one or two broad-brimmed hats of split bamboo and huge palm-leaf fans. For two mortal hours the
blue stream pours down from the steamer upon the
wharf.*

The reporter observed men arriving, only men.
Where were the Chinese women? At least half the
immigrants in those years were married men.
(Few men in China over the age of 20 remained
single unless they were wanderers or very poor.)
But the immigrants did not bring their wives, and
this was partly because they meant to stay only a
short while. They would work hard, pay off their
passage debts, save all they could, and then return

Women were not a common sight in San Francisco's Chinatown, where this photograph was taken in the 1890s. This woman's feet are bound in accordance with Chinese custom. (LIBRARY OF CONGRESS)

home to their villages. With the money a man sent or brought home, he would buy land and help ease his family's burden. Maybe he could even retire in comfort.

In this the Chinese were like many of the millions of immigrants who poured into the United States in the late nineteenth and early twentieth centuries. Immigrants from eastern or southern Europe arrived with the intention of one day going back to the familiar villages of the Old Country. They came to America mainly to make money. If things went well, they would go home with enough savings to buy a piece of land and live out their days happily. Most of these workers came to America alone; they expected to rejoin their families in Europe in a few years. A number did go back, but countless others, for various reasons, never made the return trip.

In accord with tradition, a Chinese married man left his wife in the home of his parents. Chinese custom was against wives joining their husbands overseas. Respectable women did not leave home even *with* their husbands. In those first 30 years, the United States did not restrict immigration. There was no legal barrier to the wives' coming to America. (Not until 1882 did a new law bar both Chinese men and women from entering

A Chinese woman and her children, Olympia, Washington.
(LIBRARY OF CONGRESS)

the country.) And yet very few wives came, because custom bound them to their homeland.

During the period of unrestricted immigration, some 9,000 Chinese women did make the trip to America. Many of them were kidnapped or bought in China, then sold in America as prostitutes. Some men did bring wives, but often the women could not stand the harshness of pioneer life. They died early, or returned to China. Those who survived started a family life in one or another of America's Chinatowns.

Chinatown

華僑

THEY MINED AMERICA'S gold, built her railroads, drained her swamps, and harvested her crops. But only a few of the Chinese pioneers realized their dream. In ten or 20 years a small number did well enough to return to their villages, buy land, and live out their days in some comfort. Most never earned enough to do this. They lived poorly, managed somehow to send money home regularly, but never struck it rich. Half of the 300,000 who came to America in the 30 years up to 1882 failed to make it, and returned to China to stay.

In the 1800s life in the villages of Kwangtung was so hard that most of the young men thought only of leaving for America. In some cases boys left as soon as they reached working age. The folks at home relied on them for income, and it seemed that no matter what job they found in America, the young men did better than they

These Chinese men in San Francisco's Chinatown are reading the posted bulletins about the Boxer Rebellion back home. (LIBRARY OF CONGRESS)

would have at home. Sometimes a young man saved enough to make a trip back to China. He would stay a few months, take a bride, and start a family. Then he would go back to America alone, to continue to work and send money home. Each succeeding generation of a family would try to send a man overseas. "That's the only way you can make things better," they would say.

"Sojourners"—that is the word for the Chinese immigrants who lived an in-between life. They were no longer in their homeland, but neither was America their home. They clung to the culture and ways of life of the China they had come from. They remained loyal to their families and their villages, were friendly with the immigrants from their clan or village and distant from the other people in the community.

How did the Chinese sojourner look at America? One student of Chinese-American life, Stanford M. Lyman, writes:

Typically, he is neither hostile nor despairing; rather he regards the conditions of his long lonely existence as a challenge to wit and patience. The overseas American society exists for him as a job and an opportunity, not as something to reject, rebuke, or revolt against. To the sojourner his own primary group—kin and friends in China—are the center of things. It is for them that he labors so long abroad. It is to them that he owes whatever his work may bring. It is by them that he will be honored and remembered. The sojourner is a man who remains in an alien country for a very long period of time without being assimilated by it.

That, of course, is just one side of the picture. The other side of Chinese life in America was shaped by racism. Prejudice, discrimination, humiliation—every sojourner was the victim of them. If the first Chinese immigrants did not wish to be absorbed by America, that was no reason for Americans to treat them with contempt as inferiors. The Chinese never fully adopted the ways of any new country in which they settled. For that matter, no ethnic or racial minority group is ever fully absorbed by a new world.

The sojourner's way of life stretched from America across the ocean to China. When a father in America sent for his son, probably a young teenager, he received a Chinese boy, a person far less Americanized than himself. The usual conflict between immigrant parent and child was different with the Chinese. It was the son, not the father, who knew nothing about American life and had to learn its ways.

Wishing to remain Chinese, the sojourner lived in a Chinese world in America.

Such an ethnic immigrant neighborhood was common, and still is. It was natural for newcomers to collect in a few city blocks where they could feel at home with their own. In New York City, with the great wave of immigration, a dozen different ethnic colonies sprang up. The Irish, the Germans, the Italians, the East European Jews, and many others each had their own districts. The choice in such cases was not entirely up to the individual. Discrimination forced people into ghettos even if they wanted to live elsewhere. But in a ghetto the immigrant was surrounded by people from his native land; he did not lose touch with his country and his culture. In the streets and buildings of Chinatown, he ate, slept, worked, and played guided by his Chinese tastes and values. He remained a man from Kwangtung or Fukien even while living in San Francisco, New York, or Boston, or in some small town.

The Chinatowns of America were all quite small districts. In San Francisco, the first immigrants settled within the bounds of Kearny and

Stockton, Sacramento and Jackson streets. The Chinese quarter grew somewhat, but until the earthquake of 1906, it never covered more than 15 blocks.

In its early years, San Francisco was full of small hotels, rooming houses, and flophouses occupied largely by single men who had come west to make their fortunes. As the Chinese began to arrive, the landlords sliced their rooms into smaller ones to get more rent out of their buildings. The landlords' action forced the Chinese to live in more cramped and miserable quarters than they might otherwise have.

When the Chinese spread beyond the West Coast, they started Chinatowns in the neighborhoods of many other cities. As we have seen, the first Chinese were nearly all men. They were bound by tradition not to bring wives with them to America. And later, restrictive laws forbade the immigration of wives. So for 80 years, from 1850 to the 1930s, the Chinatowns were made up mostly of men. When Chinese men at last began to bring their families to America, the Chinatowns changed. But living conditions did not get much better. Jade Snow Wong takes us into her San Francisco home, where her father made men's and children's denim clothing:

He leased sewing equipment, installed machines in a basement where rent was cheapest, and there he and his family lived and worked. There was no thought that dim and airless quarters were terrible conditions for living and working, or that child labor was unhealthful. The only goal was for all in the family to work, to save, and to become educated. It was possible, so it would be done. . . .

We lived on both levels of our factory, which had moved out of the basement to street level. The kitchen, bathroom and sitting room–dining room were at the rear of the street floor. Kitchen privileges were granted employee seamstresses, who might wish to heat lunch or wash hands; our family practically never had privacy. . . . Bedrooms were upstairs, both in the front and the rear of the factory, to be where there were windows. Between front and rear bedrooms were more machines and the long cutting tables, which were partially lit by the skylights. I shared a room with my younger sister, and later with my baby brother, too. Windows were fitted with opaque glass to eliminate the necessity for curtains, and iron bars were installed by Daddy across the entire length of those upstairs windows to keep out intruders and keep in peeping children. . . . There was little time for play, and toys were unknown to me.

For most working men in Chinatown, life was hard. Their main concern was just to survive.

Two researchers, Victor and Brett Nee, inter-
viewed hundreds of aged Chinese to record their
memories of their early days in San Francisco.
Here they sum up what they learned:

*The men remember the difficult search for employ-
ment, long hours of work, the small, crowded rooms
where they lived with their cousins, two or three beds
nailed one above another, like shelves, onto the walls.
They remember periods when the room was so crowded
that even those beds had to be used in shifts by the men
going back and forth to work. They remember hauling
crates from the streets of Chinatown up to the rooms to
use as tables and cabinets, and where there was no gas
or electricity for heating and cooking, the crates were
used as firewood. . . .*

*At the end of the year, men living in the room would
gather together to total their expenses and divide them.
Some of the funds were used to keep a bed open in the
room constantly for those who had no work. Another
allotment was spent to keep a sack of rice in the room
for the unemployed men. . . .*

*For entertainment, the men remember long nights
visiting each other's rooms. They played mah jong, and
storytelling was a highly respected art. Almost any subject provided an opportunity to display one's skill as a
debater. . . . On free days when it was still light and the*

Chinese workingmen often lived in small, crowded quarters.

*weather was good, they would stroll around Chinatown
or maybe gather in Portsmouth Square. . . .*

Some Chinese immigrants had to live and work
by themselves, away from any Chinatown. Sur-
rounded by whites, they kept to themselves. The
language barrier was one reason for this. Another
was the reluctance of prejudiced whites to reach
out to a stranger. But there was also the men's
own desire simply to do the job at hand until they
could save enough to return home.

In his novel *The Marginal Man,* L. C. Tsung tells
us something of this lonely life in a passage about
a Chinese laundryman:

*The neon sign of a Chinese hand laundry reminded
Charles of the several shirts he had not yet picked up. The
sign said Wen Lee, but Charles had never been able to
ascertain whether the proprietor's family name was Wen
or Lee. He entered the shop and saw the old man still
hard at work behind the counter, ironing under a naked
electric bulb, although it was already ten o'clock at
night. . . .*

*"How many years have you been in the States?"
Charles asked out of curiosity as he paid the man.*

"Forty years," the old man answered in Cantonese,

and raised four fingers. . . . No expression showed on his face.

"Do you have a family?"

"Big family. A woman, many sons and grandsons. All back home in Tangshan."

"Have you ever gone back since you came out here?"

"No, I only send money," replied the old man. From underneath the counter he brought out a photograph and showed it to Charles. In the center sat a white-haired old woman, surrounded by some fifteen or twenty men, women, and children of various ages. . . . The whole clan, with contented expressions on their faces, were the off-spring of this emaciated old man, who supported not only himself but all of them by his two shaking, bony hands. They seemed to represent the flow of a great river of life, originating from a tiny stream. The stream may dry up some day, but the river flows on. The old man put on his glasses . . . and identified each person in the picture to Charles Lin. A toothless smile came to his expressionless face.

Charles Lin realized that this picture was the old man's only comfort and relaxation. He had toiled like a beast of burden for forty years to support a large family which was his aim of existence, the sole meaning of his life. The picture to him was like a diploma, a summa cum laude to an honor student. Behind the fa-cade of sadness and resignation there was the inner satis-

faction which made this old man's life bearable and meaningful.

The old way of life in China was carried into the new world by the immigrants. China was a society organized into many associations. These took root in America, too. In America, the immigrants joined their clan groups or their territorial groups.

The Chinese merchants who won success in Chinatown became the upper class. They led the immigrant associations, handed out jobs, settled disputes, and acted as spokesmen for the Chinese in all affairs. Chinatown was run by this unofficial government to a considerable degree.

Each clan or family group in Chinatown grew up around a leading merchant's store. Such a self-made man of the ghetto was usually the clan's chief. Above his store was a place for kinsmen to stay when they arrived. He offered the newcomers advice and aid, and provided comfort and shelter. The clan reminded the immigrant of his obligations to the village and the family back in China. The clan leaders were something like foster parents to the newcomer. Few of these merchant leaders became rich by American standards; they were small businessmen.

Each clan in Chinatown also operated as an economic brotherhood or guild. Each clan concentrated on a trade, on the manufacture of one kind of product, or on some branch of labor. The members of one clan might own mostly fruit and candy stores. Another clan would specialize in restaurants. In some Chinatowns, a single clan won leadership; in others, two or more shared it. In San Francisco's Chinatown, the biggest and most powerful clans were the Won, Lee, and Chin families.

With the great changes that took place in Chinese-American life after World War II, the clans began to lose some of their power. Later generations of Chinese Americans often did not register with their clans. The mutual aid once provided for the elderly and the poor gave way to government welfare programs. Seeing their membership shrink, some clans began to provide new kinds of services to recover their strength. They opened recreational facilities, offered scholarships, made loans for new business ventures, and started women's divisions.

Larger than the clans were the associations uniting the Chinese Americans by the places they came from. These district associations, called *hui*

The spread of Chinese-American enterprise throughout the western United States is evidenced by this business directory. (WELLS FARGO BANK HISTORY ROOM)

kuan, were in some ways like the hometown associations other immigrants formed. The East European Jews, for example, had their *landsmanshaften* made up of Jews from the same village or neighborhood in the Old Country. The members helped one another with loans, sickness benefits, funeral costs, and burial plots. They felt better about helping members of their own group than about accepting charity from outsiders. The landsmanshaften also served the immigrants' deep need to join with family and friends to strengthen the ties to the Old Country.

The Chinese groups, however, had greater power over their members and served more functions than the landsmanshaften. Almost all the Chinese who entered California joined an association. The *hui kuan* represented their members in dealings with other associations and with the white people as well. They settled differences among their members, avoiding violent conflicts or intervention by the courts. Through the services they performed, they controlled many aspects of their members' lives. Loyalty to the association was demanded of the Chinese. Anyone who turned his back on his group was almost certain to be punished.

In San Francisco, several such district groups

joined together in the 1850s to form the Chinese Consolidated Benevolent Association (CCBA). They became known as the Chinese Six Companies, although later they expanded to embrace many more groups. They dominated community life inside Chinatown and spoke for it to American officials. Defending the Chinese from outside threats, the CCBA could unite and act decisively, but often it was split by jealousies and rivalries among Chinatown's many groups. From the 1850s on, the CCBA worked to protect the Chinese against prejudice and discrimination, fighting against unjust laws and practices. It was hard to make progress, however, against the overwhelming waves of racial hatred.

Not everything about the CCBA was "benevolent." San Francisco's Chinatown was largely a closed society inside the big city. And city, state, and federal officials let the CCBA run it like a foreign colony. Often the interests of the merchant leaders were in conflict with those of the common members. The CCBA's control over jobs, trade, debts, and disputes gave it the power to exploit the people of Chinatown, who sometimes rebelled against it.

In the 1960s, the militant American-born youth of Chinatown started to criticize the groups that ran the CCBA. Investigations revealed that the services they offered in Chinatown were inadequate, and that the sick and the poor were neglected. The result was a weakening of their traditional authority. The *hui kuan* have remained active, but the rights and privileges of the older leaders are no longer as great or numerous as they once were. To survive, the associations have had to adapt to the needs and demands of the younger Chinese Americans.

Many of the early immigrants from southeastern China were members of secret societies. There were several such societies in the homeland, some of them hundreds of years old. They drew people who no longer had a place in the clan or village organizations. The clans often quarreled with one another, and landlords fought with tenants, the poor rebelled against the rich, villages battled with imperial officials. Such clashes produced rebels, people ousted from clan or village, adventurers, and disappointed office seekers. In secret societies these people found a place where they could band together for many purposes.

Through a secret society, the discontented could protest against injustice. Peasants or workers might start their own secret group, or join an existing one. In times when the government had little popular support, such societies flourished. Like the Robin Hood of legend, a secret society might rob the rich and pass some of the loot on to the poor. A secret society might join or lead a revolt against the rulers. But most secret societies were not revolutionary. Instead, they sold strong-arm services to landlords and criminal chiefs. They became a kind of private police force that "protected" vice and crime, and put down upris-ings by the poor and oppressed.

Overseas, the Chinese formed chapters of their homeland secret societies, or started new ones. They signed up members not by clan or district ties, but on the basis of some common grievance or need. In America, the groups became known as *tongs.* Every Chinatown has had them. Some have taken part in homeland politics by offering aid to one political force or another.

The secret societies in America did not fight white racism or anti-Chinese legislation. Their energies were directed against the power of the clans and the *hui kuan.* They became rallying points for anyone discontented with Chinatown's controlling groups. What gave the secret societies a solid base was their role in criminal activities.

By the 1860s they controlled the drug traffic (in opium and other narcotics) within San Francisco's Chinatown, and they managed its gambling houses and prostitution.

The early Chinese immigrants were forced to live a lonely and frustrated bachelor life in America. They were cut off from most of the recreation that white settlers could enjoy. So they found their few pleasures where they could.

Gambling was one of those pleasures. It was common in China, and easy to continue to enjoy in America, where it was equally common among whites. It brought men together in this home that was not a home. And, like the people living in most ghettos, the Chinese hoped that gambling part of their wages would lift them out of poverty. The right bet, a good draw in the lottery, or success with cards or dominoes could bring the money a man needed to go back to China in style. So it became a social pleasure that filled lonely evenings. Behind laundries, above shops or restaurants, in rooming houses, or in basement rooms below street level, men gathered to play the games they had known back home—*f'an t'an, pai kop piu, bok-a-bau, gee fah,* and *mah jong.*

Prostitution was a result of the far greater number of men than women in Chinatown. In the

1850s, Chinese women began arriving in California in small numbers. Most of them were not the wives or daughters of the sojourners, but women kidnapped in their homeland, or bought as slaves, and then carried to America to be sold as prostitutes. They were kept as prisoners. If they tried to escape, the police and courts were bribed to return them. The prostitutes were valuable "properties," for lonely Chinese men would pay well for their services.

The secret societies profited from supplying such illegal services as gambling and prostitution. When the secret societies competed with one another for control of these illegal services in Chinatown, it led to gang wars and killings. Like the gangs of other ethnic groups, the secret societies hired gunmen, called "highbinders" or "hatchet men." The thugs were promised protection—money until they were well if they were wounded, and their families would receive money if they were killed. When they were caught by the police and tried in court, the secret societies furnished perjured testimony to get them off. *Tong* warfare seems to have faded in the 1930s. But secret societies still exist in American Chinatowns.

The Question of Color

華僑

HERE WE ARE, more than halfway along in the story of the Chinese Americans, and what comes up again and again? The question of color. Wherever the Chinese immigrant goes in America, whatever he does, his color is the first thing whites see. If his skin were black, brown, or red, it would be the same. The Chinese newcomer is seen as nonwhite. And not being white, he is in trouble.

Why should color matter so much? What makes white people so anxious about nonwhite peoples?

Racism was already rampant in Europe 300 years ago. It is the belief that the various human races have certain inborn characteristics that determine their cultures. Usually people who hold this mistaken belief are convinced that their own race is superior and therefore has the right to rule others. Such a notion made it easy to justify the enslavement of Africans. They were not white, but black, and therefore inferior, the argument ran. Africans couldn't take care of themselves. They needed the kind care of the "great white father." That assumption was repeated over and over again.

When Thomas Jefferson wrote, "All men are created equal," he was almost certainly not thinking of blacks. He and many of the Founding Fathers held the common racist belief in the superiority of whites. The American Revolution was fought for independence and freedom, but when the war ended, slavery still went on. Worse, it spread to new territories.

Hunger for more land drove settlers south and west. Expansion was all very well if nothing or no one stood in the way of it. But there were Indians on those new lands. They were nonwhite, and therefore considered inferior. From the time of Columbus, white explorers and colonizers saw the Indians as barbaric heathens in need of conversion to Christianity. Or they saw them as scarcely human, as objects to be enslaved or pushed out of the way, and, if they resisted, to be trampled over and killed. By the time the Chinese began to arrive by the thousands in the 1850s, the Indians were greatly reduced in number by disease and warfare, and many of the survivors were penned in on reservations.

It was not much different for the Mexicans. They stood in the way of expansion just as the Indians had. Armed white settlers lopped off the vast Texas territory from Mexico in order to extend slavery, and then plunged into war with Mexico to get still more land for slavery. The Americans launched the Mexican War with the conviction that the Mexicans were an inferior people. "An ignorant and degenerate race," wrote an American army officer, that "the Anglo-American race" would either wipe out or rule over "with republican simplicity and justice." A war against such an inferior people, wrote a newspaper editor, would be "full of fun and frolic."

It was a war that Ulysses S. Grant, who fought in it as a young West Point graduate, called the most disgraceful war the country ever fought. (This was said, to be sure, before the war in Vietnam.) And it forced the Mexicans to surrender such an enormous piece of their land that the size of the United States was nearly doubled overnight.

California was a big piece of territory already taken from Mexico in 1846 by John Charles Frémont's famous "Bear Flag Revolt" and ships of the United States Navy. The thousands of "forty-niners" who rushed to California seeking gold came mostly from the free states of the North and Midwest. Some were native-born Americans; the majority were European immigrants and their children. They saw to it that California entered the Union in 1850 as a free state. They were against slavery because they didn't want the competition of slaves to reduce their wages and thus lower their standard of living. Many such people had no desire to interfere with slavery in the South. In fact, they worried that emancipation might put millions of free blacks in competition with them for jobs. Many joined the Democratic Party, which appealed to farmers and workers while it voiced strong anti-black feelings. But few blacks lived in California at the time, so the Chinese instead became the target of the white settlers' racism.

When the Chinese pioneers arrived, the majority of Americans saw them as nonwhite, above anything else. The many differences between the American and Chinese ways of life were noticed, too, of course. But what mattered most of all to the whites was the color of the Chinese immigrants' skin.

A class of young Chinese girls at San Francisco's Chinese Mission House, an organization founded by the Presbyterian Board of Foreign Missions. (HUNTINGTON LIBRARY)

The Chinese were the first free nonwhite people to emigrate to America. They met the same anger and violence that white Americans had unleashed against the Indians, the blacks, and the Mexicans. It was a warning of bad times to come when California's newly written constitution defined the state as "for whites only." The California constitution followed the federal law of 1790, which limited the right to become naturalized citizens of the United States to "free white persons." California went on to limit the right to vote to "white, *male* citizens."

In 1850, a new California law placed nonwhite persons beyond the bounds of justice as well. "No black or mulatto person, or Indian, shall be allowed to give evidence in favor of or against a white man," read Section 14 of the Criminal Act. In 1854, a California court decision placed the Chinese in the same category as Indians and banned them from testifying in court. "Chinese, and all other people not white" were prohibited from giving evidence. In 1859, racism rolled over still another right. California closed the doors of public schools to nonwhites. To place "children of inferior races"—Chinese, blacks, and Indians—in the same classrooms with whites, the educators said, "must result in the ruin of our schools."

Taxes of many kinds were levied on the Chinese to drive them out of mining and fishing and laundries. Laws were passed to prevent corporations and public agencies from hiring them. A "Cubic Air" bill requiring a minimum space for every adult's apartment put many Chinese into San Francisco's jails. Then came a "Queue Ordinance," which required that every Chinese male prisoner have his long pigtail cut to within an inch of his scalp. Laws against interracial marriage were adopted in 30 states; many of them were directed specifically against the Chinese. In California, the law forbidding interracial marriage stood until 1948.

Step by step the Chinese were forced out of many kinds of work, hedged in by severe restrictions, and isolated from the white world. It was a pattern of racist persecution used against other peoples, too. The Southern whites hounded the emancipated slaves with restrictive "Black Codes" after the Civil War. And in Czarist Russia in the same decades, hundreds of so-called "May Laws" struck against the Jews. Everywhere this happened, hatred was unleashed and the outcome was beatings, lynchings, and the mass terror of pogroms.

This pattern has come to be known as institutional racism. Personal prejudice can do harm enough to its victims. But the Chinese, like the Indians and the blacks, suffer not only from that. What is worse is to have the whole range of society's institutions discriminate against you, segregate you, and victimize you.

Those institutions—business, the courts, the schools, the unions, the police, the press—are not abstract. They are real, they are powerful, and they are controlled by people, white people. For the Chinese who emigrated to the United States in the nineteenth century, they were instruments of torture. They worked to put the Chinese down and hold them there. The railroads, a big business institution, would not hire the Chinese until necessity forced them to. The California courts made decisions that deprived the Chinese of the elementary right of equal justice. The California schools refused to educate Chinese children. The police turned their backs when the Chinese needed protection, or even joined in mob attacks upon them. And the press? Most newspapers lied about the Chinese, spread vicious rumors about them, or demanded that they be thrown out of town or out of the country.

When the California courts told the Chinese that they could not testify, it was an open invitation to violence against them. Even before the 1854 decision the Chinese were being robbed and murdered, but following it the number of victims rapidly rose. Thieves and killers had nothing to fear —they would not be brought to justice. In just one year (1862), 88 Chinese were murdered in California. We've seen how whites, determined to drive out the Chinese miners, forced them to buy special licenses to work in the diggings. When this failed to discourage the Chinese, the white miners tried another tactic. They turned to terrorism. And of course the victims could not seek court action to protect themselves.

Some Chinese in the mining camps worked as laundrymen or cooks. Violence exploded against them, too. What happened in Rico, a Colorado camp, is an example. A midnight raid that took place in 1882 is described by the local newspaper editor:

A mob of masked men, 40 to 60, went to the Chinese laundry in the rear of Davis's old blacksmith shop, with the professed intention of running the Chinamen out of town, but it seems from their actions that plunder, robbery and the gratification of brutal desire to abuse some poor creature when completely in their power were the real motives that actuated them.

Arriving at the house, these miserable miscreants dragged the slumbering celestials from their bunks and hustled them from the house without even allowing them to put on their clothes and commenced to kick and beat them. One of them drew his pistol and shot at one of the Chinamen, the powder burning the shirt on the man's back and tearing a large hole through the garment, as well as grazing the skin on the victim's back. . . . The two Chinamen inhabiting this house were then kicked, cuffed, dragged over the ground by the hair of their heads, clubbed with pistols and sticks and otherwise maltreated and abused by their vindictive captors.

A squad was detailed to continue the punishment, while the larger portion of the gang repaired to Lee Sam's laundry on upper Glasgow Avenue. Six Chinamen resided there and were routed from their bunks in much the same manner as their brethren . . . except that no shots were fired at their place. . . . The half-naked Mongolians were thrown into the icy waters of Silver Creek. Each one of the heathens was honored and waited upon by a separate escort of still more heathenish men, and the program of kicking, cuffing, beating, etc., was carried out until the fiendish hearts of the ruffians were satisfied.

Others of the gang were busily engaged in plundering the laundries and met with very fair success. From Chang Lung's place $57 was secured. . . . At Lee Sam's

*place $413.40 was found under one of the beds and appro-
priated, of course. Many bundles of clothes, washed for
customers, as well as an overcoat, clothes and boots and
shoes belonging to the Chinese were taken. . . .*

Prejudice against the Chinese ran deep in the
working class, just as it did in other white American classes. Many workers themselves belonged
to ethnic or racial minorities. And they, too, were
targets of prejudice. But being a victim of racism
doesn't keep you from being a racist yourself. In
California, writes Roger Daniels, a student of racism, yellow and black, red and brown have, more
often than not, tried their best to keep members
of other groups on the bottom rung of the ethnic
ladder. The rivalry between the groups for jobs
and power injured them all.

Almost from the beginning, white California
laborers looked with suspicion on the Chinese
newcomers. As we've seen, white workers had the
mistaken notion that the Chinese were coolie
labor, as much a threat as black slavery. When the
railroads hired the Chinese in numbers and then
the big landowners did the same, it aroused the
anger of the unions. The unions hated companies
or enterprises that held monopolies or land or
business, and they extended that hate to the Chi-

nese, claiming that they were grabbing all the jobs, pushing out the whites, and bringing wages down. Of course the big employers preferred cheap labor, and they thought the Chinese would be easy to control. On their part, the Chinese had to take whatever work they could get in order to survive. If employers paid the Chinese low wages, it was not their fault. They were the victims, the employers the oppressors. They were not eager to work for less! To accuse them of that is like criticizing the slaves for working for nothing.

The truth is, the Chinese did not lower wages in California. It was the cheap wage rates on the East Coast that hurt labor on the West Coast. If there had been powerful national unions setting a national wage scale, wages in California would not have gone down. Nor were the Chinese "willing" victims of oppression. We saw how thousands of them struck against the Central Pacific Railroad, but lost because they were isolated and starved out. They formed labor guilds in many industries—cigars, laundries, shoes, garments— long before the whites, and they used the strike weapon to improve their conditions. One can only conclude that the Chinese worked for less when they had to. As soon as they could demand more, they did.

The prejudiced attacks upon the Chinese echo what was said about the Irish newcomers to America. (Every new ethnic group landing on our shores has heard the same outcry.) A generation before the Chinese came, it was said of the Irish that they did more work for less money than the native workingman, and lived on a lower standard, thereby decreasing wages.

While one newspaper editor attacked "the ignorant and besotted Irish," another denounced "the horde of Chinese, so degraded they can live on almost nothing." The New York *Times* asked that the Chinese be segregated on the West Coast because "their religion is wholly unlike ours, and they poison and stab. Mixing with them on terms of equality would be out of the question." Both the Irish and the Chinese were accused of "clannish exclusiveness," of "forming their own secret societies." Charges of unspeakable sin and corruption were leveled against both groups. The same things had been said, and would be said, of Germans, Italians, Jews, Poles, and other minorities.

With a difference. And that difference was that the Chinese belonged to a nonwhite race. Not only were they held undesirable on economic and cultural grounds, they could do nothing about

The cartoonist Thomas Nast depicts Miss Columbia, repre-senting the spirit of America, telling an anti-Chinese mob, "Hands off, gentlemen, America means fair play for all men." (JOHN J. APPEL AND SELMA APPEL, The Distorted Image: Stereotype and Caricature in American Popular Graphics)

their "inferior" ways because, said the white rac-
ists, those ways were passed on through the
bloodstream from generation to generation. The
Chinese could not be reformed or improved.
They could not be assimilated in the great American melting pot. They could not be "Americanized."

Soon whites were saying that if the Chinese
were allowed to stay in America and multiply,
they would do great harm to the American (meaning white) way of life. In 1871, mass demonstra-
tions against the Chinese became common. Ban-
ners appeared in the streets:

NO SERVILE LABOR SHALL POLLUTE OUR LAND
AMERICAN TRADE NEEDS NO COOLIE LABOR

The next year, in Los Angeles, a white man was
killed by a stray shot during a fight between the
police and some Chinese. A mob gathered and
invaded Chinatown with guns. Some of the
whites took positions on rooftops while others
tried to drive the Chinese out into the streets. A
spectator told what he witnessed:

*[The Chinese] were shot in their hiding places or
hunted from room to room out into the open courtyard,*

where death from the bullets of those on the roof was certain. A chorus of yells telegraphed the fact [that someone had been killed] to the surrounding mob, and the yells were answered by a hoarse roar of savage satisfaction. Men were dragged forth and hurled headlong from a raised sidewalk to the ground. To the necks of some of the most helpless the mob fastened ropes and with a whoop and a hurrah rushed down Los Angeles Street to the hanging place. A boy was thus led to the place of slaughter. The little fellow was not yet above 12 years of age. He had been but a month in the country and knew not a word of English. He was hanged.

It was midnight, and a body of men appointed by the sheriff cut down the dead. Nearly all had been dragged through the streets at the end of a rope, and all were found shot and stabbed as well as hanged.

Eighteen Chinese were murdered and many Chinese stores and homes looted and burned. Eight of the rioters, tried and found guilty, were sentenced to jail for terms of two to eight years. Within a year, all were freed.

Already rooted in Western folklore was the belief that it was no crime to kill a Chinese. A report on the Chinese of San Francisco by the city's Board of Supervisors said, "The beasts of the field, the vagrant dogs put to death by drowning, are vastly better worthy of our commiseration than the whole Mongolian race."

One of the worst anti-Chinese riots broke out at Rock Springs, Wyoming, in 1885. About 500 Chinese coal miners worked near the town. They were attacked by a mob of white laborers, many of them foreign-born, too. It ended with 28 Chinese dead, 15 wounded, and the eviction of the remaining Chinese from the town.

Seattle forcibly deported hundreds of Chinese by ship, and Tacoma, Washington, banished 3,000 on 24 hours' notice. For decades all Chinese people were banned from these cities. Chinese railroad workers had settled in towns in Utah, Colorado, and Nevada; in the 1880s all were expelled. Throughout the Rocky Mountain region and in dozens of California towns, the Chinese were burned out of their quarters, lynched, banished.

In the next ten years, racist strikes and mob violence cost the last Chinese their jobs as pickers and packers of California's fruits and vegetables. The Chinese abandoned their rural Chinatowns and retreated to San Francisco or to their homeland villages across the Pacific. By 1910, the Chinese had almost vanished from the labor market.

An anti-Chinese riot in Denver, 1880. (LIBRARY OF CONGRESS)

Despite repeated blows, the Chinese did not cower or crawl. They fought back bravely. In case after case they turned to the courts to defend their human rights. They never gave up fighting for the right to become naturalized citizens. In 1863, Lin Sing attacked the poll tax he was forced to pay, even though he was an alien. He took his case to the California Supreme Court and won it. The decision set a precedent for all aliens.

Yick Wo, a San Francisco laundryman, challenged an ordinance that required fire-safety licenses for laundrymen. His point was that the law was enforced only upon the city's 150 Chinese laundries; the 170 white laundries did not have to get licenses. In 1885 the United States Supreme Court ruled that while a license law was proper, its discriminatory enforcement was unjust. So Yick Wo won an important victory for equal protection under the law. Such resistance to injustice strengthened the Constitution for all Americans. "It is a great tribute to them [the Chinese] and to the court," wrote the legal scholar Charles Abrams, "that some of these decisions stand out today as landmarks of a developing democratic tradition." The victories of the Chinese became precedents for later court decisions granting blacks equality in law.

As too often happens, however, such court rulings marked progress only in principle, not in fact. The decisions were not respected by the states or communities. The prejudice did not end, the abuses went on, the violence continued. So hopeless did the situation of the Chinese in America seem that the phrase "Not a Chinaman's chance!" entered the language.

What made the condition of the Chinese even worse was the employers' use of them to break strikes by white workers. That was how the first Chinese got jobs in San Francisco's boot and shoe industry in 1869; they were hired in place of whites on strike. The next year, 75 Chinese were imported to work in a shoe factory in North Adams, Massachusetts. The boss announced he would use them to break the power of the shoe workers' union. "Coolie slavery!" trumpeted the press, and asked why the President did not keep them out. Soon another group of Chinese arrived in New Jersey to man a steam laundry, and white workers got panicky. "Coolies," they said, were heading for the potato fields, the railroad yards, and the cigar factories.

It was not a new story. Blacks, too, shut out by the unions, were forced to take any jobs to live, and they, too, were used as strikebreakers. So were the new immigrants from eastern and southern Europe. The unions failed to recruit the Chinese and other immigrants, and used racist arguments to defend their policy. Then, when immigrant labor broke strikes, white labor took it as proof of the rightness of their views. They were blind to the truth: that only the unity and solidarity of *all* working people would protect labor's rights and gains.

The most bitter outbursts against the Chinese rose from the American labor movement. Samuel Gompers, himself an immigrant, was the leader of the American Federation of Labor. He drew a line between immigrants he said could be assimilated and those who could not. "The Chinese? Never!" he would say time and again. He never tried to organize them. He wrote vicious racist attacks upon the Chinese, and worked hard for the total exclusion from the United States of both Chinese and Japanese.

Gompers, the loudest voice in a chorus of labor leaders, was a conservative in politics. But many radicals as well—people who favored drastic political and economic changes—spoke out against the Chinese. They included Wendell Phillips, T. V. Powderly, John Swinton, Henry George, Victor Berger, and Eugene V. Debs. Even black delegates to the first Colored State Labor Convention in Baltimore in 1869 voted in favor of keeping the Chinese out of America.

"The Chinese must go!" became a national rallying cry.

Attacks upon the Chinese were urged at rallies of the Workingmen's Party in San Francisco. (LIBRARY OF CONGRESS)

"*The Chinese Must Go!*"

華僑

CALIFORNIA'S POLITICIANS QUICKLY tuned in to the fierce sound of anti-Chinese voices.

They began to use racist hatred as bait for votes.

A new political party—the Workingmen's Party—sprang up in San Francisco in the terrible depression years of the 1870s. It was led by Denis Kearney, an Irish immigrant who worked as a teamster. There was no public welfare policy for the poor and the unemployed in those times; most Americans were interested only in the pursuit of money. Politicians like Kearney could play on the fears of men bewildered and beaten by hard times. Sharing their racism, he inflamed their feelings to win their votes. The Chinese became his victims.

The Chinese were not to blame for labor's troubles. They did not monopolize the land, they did not run the corporations, they did not bring about the depression. No matter—Kearney blamed them for everything that was wrong.

When California decided to draft a new constitution, Kearney's party put forth a program and elected delegates to the constitutional convention. Kearney's program contained many good proposals that would benefit labor. But he made opposition to the Chinese the main issue, knowing it was the easiest way to rouse passions and win victories. All the proposals dealing with the Chinese violated human rights. Yet they were taken seriously at the convention, and were adopted almost unanimously. Thus the injustices already suffered by the Chinese were stamped with the approval of the state of California and its voters.

To understand how this could happen, we need to look at what was happening in America at the time. The country's population was changing rapidly. America was turning from the agricultural society of the pre–Civil War era into a great industrial power. The cities were swelling with people moving in from the countryside and small towns. And a tidal wave of new immigrants from southern and eastern Europe was flooding American ports.

The increase in population was not only huge, it was frightening to older Americans, for the millions of new immigrants were not Europeans of familiar stock. They were strangers of many different ethnic groups. Their odd ways and tongues seemed to threaten the country's basic institutions. The old nativism—fear and distrust of newcomers—was revived. The dominant white Anglo-Saxon Protestants were alarmed. They labeled the newcomers inferior, called them "garbage" dumped on American shores.

In hard times, people stunned by their troubles tend to make scapegoats of the foreign and the weak. In the depression of the 1870s, this was true not only of workers, who feared that the newcomers would be willing to work for next to nothing and would take away their jobs, but also of those who had recently arrived in the middle class. They had sweated to get where they were, and were frantic to keep what they had. They responded hysterically when anyone played on their fears.

In the 1870s, the Socialist Party was first organized in America. Its members were mostly immigrants. Weak as the party was, its talk of class war scared the rich and the middle class. Uncontrolled immigration was blamed for letting these "foreign agitators" in. In 1877, nationwide strikes by railroad workers enraged by savage wage cuts climaxed in street battles with state troops. The spreading riots were blamed on foreign radicals.

So when Kearney began his racist assault upon the Chinese in California, it was part of the anti-foreign fever gripping the country. Again and again Kearney cried out, "The Chinese must go!" He had gotten into California's new constitution a ban on Chinese immigration. It was invalid—such matters had once been the concern of the individual states, but were no longer; only Congress had the right to regulate immigration. And the Burlingame Treaty of 1868 between China and the United States allowed the people of each country to go freely to the other. But union leaders pressed the government to change the treaty so Chinese immigration could be banned. In 1880, the treaty was amended; now the United States could suspend Chinese immigration when it wished.

That marked a deep change in American thinking. What had long been a right became a privilege. In the original Burlingame Treaty, the United States and China agreed to the inalienable right of people to cross national boundaries and change their place of habitat. But in revising the Burlingame Treaty, the United States showed that it no longer believed that the Chinese had a right to enter the country or to live here permanently. The treaty revision signaled that free immigration to the United States would soon end.

The first barrier was put up quickly. In 1882, Congress passed the Chinese Exclusion Act. It suspended the immigration of Chinese laborers for ten years. And it decreed that the Chinese who were already in the United States were forever barred from becoming citizens.

With that act of Congress, open immigration to America was ended. The Chinese became the first people to be shut out on ethnic grounds. Almost no one opposed the exclusion bill. Why?

First of all, the Chinese were not citizens. They had no vote, no power to influence decisions vital to their own welfare. Racism and lack of political strength meant they had no friends in Congress, no one to use power in their behalf. So they became a helpless pawn in political bargains. Southern Congressmen wanted support for legislation to keep down the millions of blacks in their region. Western Congressmen wanted support for measures to get rid of the Chinese in their region.

Both the Democratic and Republican parties took advantage of nationwide American prejudice against the Chinese. (LIBRARY OF CONGRESS)

Each group agreed to vote for the other's racist bills. Both national parties—the Republicans and the Democrats—knew that feeling against the Chinese was nationwide. It was easy to give in to that prejudice, and vote for the Exclusion Act, especially when the victims had no power to fight back.

Still another act restricting Chinese immigration was passed in 1888. The Scott Act said Chinese temporarily out of the country could not return. That law kept thousands of men who were visiting their families in China from coming back to America.

An amendment to the Exclusion Act permitted a man from China to enter the United States, but only if he could show papers proving he had a wife, child, or parent here. A small number of "privileged" people—merchants, teachers, clergymen, or professional Chinese—could come in, too. The amendment led at once to the buying of fake documents that would "prove" a man had a wife, child, father, or mother in the United States. Such imaginary people became known as "paper relatives."

Coming into the United States with fake documents was illegal, of course, but many Chinese entered that way. Other Chinese got in by more

While American legislation increasingly restricted Chinese immigration in the late nineteenth century, some Chinese continued to enter illegally across the Canadian or Mexican border. This cartoon points to British Columbia in Canada as the dangerous hole in the door that had not been bolted firmly enough by Congress. (JOHN J. APPEL AND SELMA APPEL, The Distorted Image: Stereotype and Caricature in American Popular Graphics)

dangerous methods. Some were smuggled across the Canadian or Mexican borders.

The Geary Act of 1892 extended all anti-Chinese legislation for ten years. And the Chinese in the United States were required to carry photo passports at all times to prove their right to be here.

What did these laws do to the Chinese-American population?

The fact that no more Chinese would be allowed in did not satisfy the many who hated the Chinese. In the West, as we've seen, the violence got even worse after the passage of the exclusion acts. Riots, burnings, looting, and the massacring of Chinese went on into the 1920s. "They call it exclusion," said Chang Kiu Sing in 1904, "but it is not exclusion, it is extermination."

Before the first exclusion act, about 300,000 Chinese entered the United States. By 1882, the majority had gone back to China. A sizeable minority remained, but for the next 40 years, or more, the Chinese population in the United States never got above 100,000. Those with enough money went back to China. Many, as we have seen, were killed in outbreaks of terrorism and violence. Those who remained found refuge in the Chinatowns of the big cities. They stayed within their neighborhoods, for often if they were seen outside, it meant a beating by whites.

With wives kept from entering the country and interracial marriage a crime, the Chinese men still in the United States had to remain single. In 1920, there were 675 Chinese males to every 100 females. Not until 1943 did that sex ratio move toward a more normal balance. Among the elderly Chinese today there is still a shortage of women as a legacy of the long years of exclusion.

Immigration officials harassed the Chinese relentlessly. They were detained and grilled, and thousands were deported on petty technicalities. Children and wives were often shipped back while husbands were let in. The ordeal was terrible. Ng Poon Chew, the editor of a Chinese newspaper in San Francisco, repeated what Chang had said in 1908: "The Exclusion Law has been carried out with such vigor that it has almost become an extermination law."

In 1924, Congress passed a new Immigration Act. It kept out all Chinese, including the wives and children of Chinese people already living here. And it banned immigrants from any other country in Asia. A whole continent of peoples was declared inferior to the Americans.

The pain and humiliation caused by exclusion laws is expressed by Connie Young Yu:

[It] was to make reunions in America virtually impossible even for those who were willing to endure the hardships. . . . In every Chinese American family history there are stories of lives made miserable by the immigration laws, harassment and fear: the lonely old single men in condemned hotel rooms, the suicides of deportees, the fragmented families. I remember being told frequently how lucky my father's father had been because he came to America in 1881, a 12-year-old laborer, just a year before the Exclusion Act. My mother's mother had a less fortunate story: though the wife of an American citizen, she was detained upon her arrival in 1920 on a health technicality and held prisoner on Angel Island (in San Francisco Bay) for two years.

The 1924 law was not changed until 1943, when China was America's ally in World War II. It would have looked foolish or crazy to continue shutting out the Chinese while we were fighting side by side with them against a common enemy. So Congress voted to end the Chinese exclusion laws and to allow the Chinese who were living here—the sojourners—to become citizens. The government set an annual immigration quota of 105 persons of Chinese ancestry, regardless of birthplace.

The Chinese had waited a long time: it had taken America 61 years to open the door again after the first exclusion act. But it was not opened very wide—the quota of 105 was one of the lowest set for any group. And while the quotas set for other peoples were based on their country of origin, for the Chinese the quota was based on race.

At the very time the 1943 law was adopted, the United States was committing a racist outrage against another Asian minority. By order of President Franklin D. Roosevelt, 110,000 men, women, and children of Japanese ancestry—two-thirds of them native-born Americans with full citizenship rights—were penned up in relocation camps in the West. The excuse was that the country was at war with Japan, and these people might give aid to the enemy. We were also at war with Germany and Italy, yet Americans of German and Italian ancestry were not being confined behind barbed wire. Making the Japanese Americans prisoners in their own country was an action taken solely on the grounds of race.

In the years after World War II, various laws were passed that added to the number of Chinese who could enter the country. Some of these were wives of Americans serving in the armed forces. Others were physicians, scientists, and people with skills that the United States decided it needed. These people were let in together with their families.

Deeper change did not come until the 1960s, when the great civil rights movement was transforming the country. Other minorities, inspired by the example of the blacks, demanded equal rights and full freedom for *all* Americans. Like the blacks, native Americans, Hispanic Americans, and Asian Americans renewed their pride in their ethnic heritage and mustered their strength to eliminate every form of institutional discrimination.

In 1962, the quota limiting the number of Chinese immigrants to 105 per year was lifted. President John F. Kennedy signed an order admitting refugees from Communist China. In 1965, President Lyndon B. Johnson abolished all laws limiting immigration on the basis of race or nationality. The act raised to 20,000 per year the quota for each Asian country—the same number set for European countries. The racial distinctions that had stained America's immigration policy for over 80 years were at last wiped out.

Large numbers of Asian people could now freely enter the United States and acquire American citizenship through naturalization. It started a fresh flow of Chinese immigration that matched the high flow of the mid-nineteenth century, in the time before the first exclusion act. At the end of the 1970s, the number of Chinese Americans had grown to about 500,000.

Pictures in the Air
華僑

Chink, Chink, Chinaman, sitting on a rail,
Along comes a white man and cuts off his tail. . . .

I LEARNED TO chant those lines when I was a child. The sound and rhythm were pleasing to my ears, and the picture the rhyme called up in my mind seemed very funny. I had no idea why a Chinese man wore his hair in a long queue. Nor did I stop to think about a white man doing something sneaky or mean to a yellow man. I must have taken for granted that there was nothing wrong with it.

Did I know any Chinese people myself? No. In the place where I grew up—it was Worcester, a Massachusetts town—I saw Chinese people rarely. Thinking back on it, it was always a Chinese man, never a woman or child. The only place I remember seeing a Chinese man was at a Chinese laundry. I looked at him through the window. (We didn't take our wash to a laundry; my mother did it at home.) I can recall peering through the glass at a man in the back of a small store. He was busy ironing a shirt or a sheet. He looked up for a moment, caught my eye, and went on working.

I was drawn to stop and stare because, I think, the Chinese seemed so strange and mysterious a people. And a little scary, too. I learned nothing about them in school. We studied American history, we studied the Greeks and the Romans. But textbooks and teachers paid no attention to Asia. Oh, I heard about the Chinese when I read of Marco Polo's travels. (That was mostly *his* story, though, not theirs.) And sometimes the newspapers had accounts of floods or famine or fighting in China. . . .

Then where did I pick up what notions I had about the Chinese? Mostly from popular music, movies, books, comics, and what I heard other people say. I remember listening to the radio and hearing such songs as "Chinatown My Chinatown," "China Boy," and "Little Chinky Butterfly." Behind the words were meanings I didn't think about.

My gang went to the movies on Saturdays. We

saw lots of pictures—Westerns, mysteries, comedies, horror stuff. Every once in a while a movie would have Chinese people in it. I can remember Lon Chaney as the evil Mr. Wu, and Boris Karloff as the frightening Dr. Fu Manchu. The films, like the songs, planted something in my mind about the Chinese.

What? A picture of them as a group, a people who all looked the same and who all behaved the same. "Chink" was the name everyone called them. It was like the names tagging other groups —nigger, mick, wop, Polack, kike, gook, Jap, honky, spic. Names that expressed feelings—of contempt, fear, hatred. They called up a definite image—a hostile one.

There's a word for such an image—"stereotype." It means a judgment that does not match the facts. It's an illusion—a false, not a true, picture of reality. A stereotype stamps all members of a group of people with certain features that they are all supposed to have. (A stereotype is most powerful if the people stereotyped have some badge we easily recognize them by. Color is the easiest one.)

When I believed all Chinese were evil and scary, it was not because I knew any Chinese and saw them do evil or scary things. It was because

This figurine helped to spread the racist stereotype. The Chinese man, wearing a pigtail and clutching a tea kettle and opium pipe, sits astride a rat, which symbolizes his alleged diet of dogs and vermin. The image was part of the "Cupids of All Nations" series in Life *magazine.* (JOHN J. APPEL AND SELMA APPEL, The Distorted Image: Stereotype and Caricature in American Popular Graphics)

this picture of them was "in the air." By that I mean it was deep in the culture I grew up with. The stereotype was in the songs, the doggerel, the movies, the stories. It was in the jokes, the offhand remarks, the expressions of the older people around me.

There is a telltale likeness in the stereotypes of dozens of racial and ethnic groups. The stereotype about black Americans, for instance, holds that they are shiftless, dirty, can't learn, won't work, and lower living standards and property values. The same things were said in California in the 1930s about the so-called "Okies." These were white farmers who were driven off their lands by the Great Depression. They went to California to seek work on the fruit and vegetable farms. They were called lazy and shiftless and irresponsible. Why? Because the people they worked for—those who owned or managed the farms—wanted to keep them down.

So it was with the Chinese when they began coming to America. They were stereotyped in American minds *before* they arrived. How did that affect the Chinese? Think of it this way: all around us is the buzzing confusion of the world. When I look at a new person, my mind doesn't see that person purely as himself and then tell me what it has seen. No, when I look at someone, my mind contains what our culture has told me about him. If he is dressed shabbily, I am more likely to jump to the conclusion that he is poor than that he is dressed for cleaning out the basement. Which means, in this case, that white Americans tended to see the Chinese in a stereotyped way. They weren't aware of doing this, they didn't think about it, they just reacted in an almost mechanical way.

Soon Americans' negative view of the Chinese was thickened by other notions—that the Chinese were "only fit for" certain types of work, that they could live on next to nothing, that they were meek and docile, that they couldn't be trusted, that they were opium fiends, filthy, diseased, etc.

No wonder that when a study was made of what American children think about various peoples, a typical answer was: "I don't like the Chinese because they have such a bad reputation."

Let's see how such a reputation grows. Take our schoolbooks. The early geography books were mostly critical of the Chinese. And here is how one history book described them:

The Chinese have long been considered an undesirable addition to our population. Living on only a few cents a day, they are willing to work for wages which other laborers could not accept. In cities where they have settled in any number, they congregate in a "Chinatown" in which unsanitary living is combined with strange customs and low moral standards, if not crimes; it is believed they form a menace to our civilization. . . .

That's the old stereotype at work again.

Just as much harm can be done by what the textbooks leave out. Even today, many of them "forget" to mention the Chinese at all. Or they just show a picture of San Francisco's Chinatown with a caption. Most of the books don't tell the story of what the Chinese workers have done in America, of the oppressive laws and mob violence directed against them, or of their long struggle to overcome racism.

What we do for fun often affects our ideas more than schools or textbooks. Long before movies, radio, and television, Americans went to the theater for entertainment. Only a few years after the first Chinese immigrants came to America, plays with Chinese characters in them were performed. White actors put on makeup and costumes to play "John Chinaman."

This stock character was put into plays for

laughs. He wore "coolie" dress and a queue long enough to sweep the floor. The makeup exaggerated slanted eyes and yellow skin. The actor spoke in Pidgin English. This made audiences think that all Chinese spoke a curious dialect that had little to do with English. The Chinese characters' words often ended in "ee," as in "washee" and "drinkee." Words with an "r" or "th" in them were usually spoken as if they were spelled with an "l." For "d" the actor said "t." Here's an example—in a song taken from a show performed by the San Francisco Minstrels when they toured the country in the 1880s:

"The Chinee Laundryman"

Me comee from Hong Kong Chinee
To workee for de Mellican man,
Me no talkee much English,
Me speakee you de best I can.
Me workee all day in laundry,
For ching chong dat's his name,
Me catchee de rats in de market,
Makee pot-pie all a same.

CHORUS

Oh ching chong opium, taffy on a stick,
No likee brass band, makee very sick,

Mellican man listen, sing you littee song,
With a Chinee fiddle, and a Shanghai gong.

This passed for humor back in those days. The Chinese newcomers simply spoke poor English, like all the other immigrants. They mispronounced words or wrongly accented them; some western sounds were hard for them to master. But that was no excuse for Americans to make fun of them. How many Americans could speak a word of Chinese?

Popular writers also poked fun at the Chinese immigrants. Bret Harte and Mark Twain wrote a play called *Ah Sin: The Heathen Chinee.* It was the story of a Chinese laundryman on the Western frontier. Both writers thought of themselves as friendly to the Chinese. Nevertheless, their stereotyped comedy ridiculed the immigrants. The subtitle, *Heathen Chinee,* repeated a phrase that was often used to jeer at Chinese religion. In such plays, the white characters got extra laughs by casually kicking the Chinese characters or yanking at their queues.

One of the most powerful stereotypes of the Chinese was created by the writer Sax Rohmer. In 1913 he began making his Dr. Fu Manchu the villain of a long series of novels. Fu Manchu was

And he went for that heathen Chinee.

Illustrated above is a stanza from Bret Harte's popular poem, "The Heathen Chinee," the tale of a Chinese laundryman on the western frontier who also was a wily cardsharp. If Harte meant to satirize anti-Chinese prejudice, the effect upon the general public was only to strengthen the stereotype. (LIBRARY OF CONGRESS) labeled "the most diabolical, sinister and all-around un-nice Oriental mastermind of all time." His dream was to conquer Europe and America. In one of his novels, Rohmer tells of a victim of Fu Manchu held "at the mercy of this enemy of the white race, of this inhuman being who himself knew no mercy, of this man whose very genius was inspired by the cool, calculated cruelty of his race, of that race which to this day disposes of hundreds, nay thousands of its unwanted girl-children by the simple measure of throwing them down a well specially dedicated to that purpose."

In 1929, Hollywood took up Fu Manchu and made millions out of the distorted image. When Boris Karloff played Fu Manchu in the movies, the ads promised "menace in every twitch of his finger . . . terror in each split second of his slanted eyes."

The great success of the Fu Manchu books and films planted a completely prejudiced picture of the Chinese in the minds of millions of Americans. One of the phrases Rohmer often used was "the yellow menace." He had picked up an old fear first voiced in America back in the time of England's Opium Wars with China, when a rumor was spread that the Chinese were out to conquer the earth. (The truth was rather that white nations wanted economic domination over China.)

"The Yellow Peril" became a popular theme in newspapers and magazines. They carried stories about "the swarm of Chinese" ready to strike American shores in "a tidal wave which may overwhelm us." (The fact that so few Chinese were coming in as immigrants, compared with vast numbers of Europeans, didn't make any difference.) Editors scared readers with threats of a Chinese invasion like that of Genghis Khan. When the Japanese defeated the Russians in the war of 1904–05, it added to the fright. An Oriental nation had defeated a white one! The publisher William Randolph Hearst, who owned many newspapers, got especially excited about the Yellow Peril. He was one of the strongest voices braying about a Yellow Peril in his many newspapers. He even made a movie to preach the Yellow Peril gospel. Jack London, one of the most popular writers of the time, had long believed in white supremacy. Now he, too, began warning about the Yellow Peril.

The stories and films about the villain Fu Manchu were followed within a dozen years by a batch of novels, movies, and radio shows about a Chinese detective, Charlie Chan. This character

*Myrna Loy, Terrence Granville, and Boris Karloff—as Dr. Fu
Manchu—in* The Mask of Fu Manchu. (THE MUSEUM OF MODERN
ART/FILM STILLS ARCHIVE)

was not an evil menace, but a pudgy, smiling man who upheld the law. It was a change, but Charlie Chan was still portrayed as "inscrutable" and "mysterious." The old comic treatment of a Chinese person speaking English was used, and both Fu Manchu and Charlie Chan were always played by white actors. The two characters are only different facets of the same stereotype. While one is aggressively evil, the other is passive, apologetic, and accommodating. In the one case white readers and audiences could feel frightened but superior, and in the other they could feel kindly but just as superior.

Chinese women, too, have been made the victims of stereotypes by the entertainment world. A type known as the "China Doll" has often been portrayed on the stage, in the movies, and on television. Anna May Wong was the first actress to present that image—the dainty, slinky sex object who can't resist the charms of white men. The superior white males can always mix with Asian women. But Asian men are forbidden to touch white women.

Television is no different from the other media. And because it reaches many more people, its effects are far worse. One of the most popular TV Westerns, *Bonanza,* worked a Chinese cook into

Charlie Chan (right), played by Sidney Toler, with his assistant,
Number One Son, played by Sen Yung, in Charlie Chan Goes to
Panama. (THE MUSEUM OF MODERN ART/FILM STILLS ARCHIVE)

the series. This character looked, acted, and
talked much like the comic laundryman, Ah Sin,
of the Bret Harte-Mark Twain play of the 1870s.
A hundred years had passed, but the stereotype
was still alive. The only difference now was that
a Chinese actor, not a white one, played the
"funny" part.

Asian actors in recent years have fought against
stereotyped roles, and some have succeeded in
reshaping characterizations to make them honest
and true. An occasional film or TV show breaks
away from the worst stereotypes. But the advertisements we see on TV and in the press often
rely on the old racist images. The Chinese speak
Pidgin English, and they are shown as humble
and obedient. If cosmetics are being promoted, a
slinky Asian woman is shown preferring a white
man over an Asian. And the comics don't seem to
have advanced very much, either. Young people
who read them (or watch TV versions of comic-
strip stories) see ridiculous caricatures of Asians
that might well have been dreamed up 100 years
ago.

Making It?

華僑

"THEY'VE MADE IT," people say of the Chinese in America. "They've arrived, they're in."

You don't see many Chinese on the welfare rolls, people say, or picked up as juvenile delinquents. No, look at I. M. Pei, the famous architect, his picture on the cover of the New York *Times Magazine*. Or look at Y. D. Lee, Samuel Ting, and C. N. Yang, Nobel Prize winners in physics. And what about Gerald Tsai, the financier? And Hiram Fong, the United States Senator?

The Chinese are a quiet, hardworking people with no problems and no doubts. They have homes in the suburbs, children in college. The "model minority"—that's the picture painted of the Chinese Americans.

How true is it?

Before World War II, Chinese Americans' chances for enjoying a good life were slim. Some sociologists even predicted that because the Chinese were denied the chance to create families in the United States, they would soon die out. But in the 1920s and 1930s, a number of Chinese were able to start families. A small second generation began—a generation born here and educated in the public schools and in Chinese-language schools. These Chinese were raised by their parents to think of themselves as sojourners. Learn modern American ways, they were urged, and use them in China to build up the homeland.

In those years, the way up the economic ladder was closed to most Chinese. They could find work only in the businesses run by their kinfolk in America's Chinatowns. They got jobs in restaurants, laundries, curio shops, and the garment trades. Even for Chinese with college educations, careers in the professions seemed impossible. Some went off to China in the hope of making a better living there.

Then, in the 1940s, life for the Chinese in America began to open up. World War II had much to do with it.

When the war broke out, many plants making military supplies refused to hire black workers. Only the threat of a mass march on Washington got President Franklin D. Roosevelt to order an

Three generations of Chinese Americans are represented at this busy street crossing in San Francisco's Chinatown. (WIDE WORLD PHOTOS)

end to discrimination in industries holding government contracts. Still, race riots broke out because blacks felt they were not being treated fairly. They asked if the "Four Freedoms" America said it was fighting for were reserved for whites only. Blacks were segregated and discriminated against in the armed forces. Over a million black men and women served in World War II. But not until the last year of the war did integration of black and white troops begin.

As the war progressed and a shortage of white labor developed, many black workers got jobs in the new defense industries. But they were segregated in housing, on buses and trains, in schools, in unions. Washington, D.C., the nation's capital, was as segregated a town then as Pretoria, South Africa, is today.

Protest organizations took to the picket lines and the courts in a fight for equality. Finally, in 1954, a sweeping decision by the United States Supreme Court ruled that the schools could no longer be segregated. The court decision meant even more than that. It meant that American law no longer stood for the proposition that blacks were inferior to whites. With that decision, the legal structure whites had built to deny the civil rights and the humanity of all colored peoples began to crumble. It was a powerful shot fired in the struggle to achieve a just American society.

In the postwar years a great many white Americans, especially the young, awoke to what a terrible burden racism is. They joined with all the minorities in a broad civil rights movement. Together they won the passage of many civil rights laws. Chinese Americans, like other racial and ethnic groups, for the first time tasted the sweet prospect of full equality.

World War II had given the Chinese, too, a chance at blue-collar and white-collar jobs that had been closed to them in the past. As the civil rights movement gathered force, old discriminatory laws were struck down. In 1947, the restrictive covenants that had kept Chinese people from buying homes in San Francisco outside of Chinatown were lifted. Now those who had better jobs with good pay could move into other neighborhoods of the city. A year later, California's antimiscegenation law was repealed—interracial marriage was no longer illegal. In 1952, the California Supreme Court tossed out the old state law barring Orientals from owning land. The first federal low-rent housing for Chinese Americans was erected in the 1950s. In 1964, Title VII of the federal Civil Rights Act barred discrimination in employment. It required companies with government contracts to pursue an affirmative action program for hiring, recruiting, training, and promoting members of minority groups.

What made opportunities greater for Chinese Americans was not simple goodwill. True, white Americans had begun to see China and the Chinese Americans in a more favorable light during World War II. But it took a mass civil rights movement to break up the old American pattern of racism. The Chinese Americans were ready to do their share in the fight for civil rights because of the change in their population that began in the 1940s. Not only were Chinese allowed to immigrate from 1943 on; young people from China were also allowed in for higher education. They were not laborers from Kwangtung, but came from China's upper class. Their American educations were meant to prepare them for top jobs in Nationalist China. When the Communist revolution triumphed in China in 1949, the Chinese students were stranded here. The United States allowed them to stay on and work. Many became permanent residents. Later, other students entered from Hong Kong and Taiwan.

Within 20 years, more than 50,000 Chinese immigrated to the United States. The majority of

The Chinese Americans are one of many minority groups that have banded together to secure their equal rights. (CORKY LEE)

them were women, and many of these women
were the wives of citizens. This influx of women
raised the birthrate and strengthened family life.
Young Chinese Americans, especially, began to
explore their roots and to study their American
past. This led to a renewed sense of identification
with the Chinese community. Chinese Americans
began to value what was different about themselves and to assert their right to their uniqueness.
They demanded a fair share of the federal funds
allocated to meet the needs of minorities long discriminated against. They formed local and national organizations to speak for them in the political arena.

A Chinese-American middle class arose. Chinese chemists, physicists, pharmacists, dentists,
doctors, scholars, artists, architects, engineers, ac-
countants, and computer programmers have entered the professional world. Most of them are
American-born and college-educated. Schooling
was their entry to an industrial and technical society. A zest for study had ancient roots for them,
just as it did for Jewish immigrants.

Ancient Chinese cultural tradition placed the
educated man at the top of the social ladder. By
definition, the learned man was the good man.
When the opportunity for education came, it was

eagerly seized. Chinese Americans have made rapid advances in their chosen fields of study and have enriched scholarship and science. Today a greater percentage of Chinese males are college-educated than white males. And the number of Chinese males entering the professions has increased at a much greater rate than for the total American male population. The figures show that Chinese Americans as a group have moved upward more rapidly than the general population.

But while there is a new middle class, a great many Chinese are still found in low-skilled jobs. The two traditional Chinese enterprises—laundries and restaurants—are still those many work in. These laborers are often relatives of Chinatown merchants who paid their passage from Hong Kong. In return, the newcomers donate their labor for a certain time, or work at cheap rates. It becomes a kind of serfdom, with family ties so tight that a struggle for better wages or unionization is made very difficult. The immigrants feel trapped in dead-end jobs. Busboy, waiter, dishwasher, janitor—there is no place to go from there. Lillian Sing, a social worker in the Newcomers' Service of San Francisco's Chinatown, tells what happens to these workers:

I think when they first get here the immigrants have a lot of strength. . . . They have not been discouraged by too much discrimination in Hong Kong. They are used to thinking that if they try hard enough they'll make it. . . . Before they come they have this feeling that the United States has great opportunities for everyone, all you have to do is work. But when they get there they find that many things are limited. There's the language problem, limitation of jobs, and then even though they want to try very hard, they just can't make it. A lot of them don't speak English, which is a major setback.

The language barrier keeps the newcomers from finding work outside Chinatown, in American industry. With so many forced to seek a living inside, the competition for jobs drives wages down. The only choice for most is to work long hours at low pay or to go on welfare.

Danny Lowe had a painting job in Hong Kong before he came to America on money a relative lent him. He hoped to do better here, but with no education and unable to speak English, he could find work only in a Chinatown fish market. He started at seven A.M. and put in a 12-hour day. His pay was $280 a month. He soon learned that Chinese men who had been working there for 20 years never got more than $400. If they asked for more, the boss would say, "OK, you gotta go. I don't need you because I got so many people waiting for the job." It was bitter to realize he was worse off than in Hong Kong. After six years in San Francisco, Danny Lowe still hoped to get work outside Chinatown or to join an American union. There was no union in the fish market.

Nor are unions present or effective in the branch of the garment trade where most Chinese Americans find work. Sweatshops are common in the large Chinatowns of America—in New York, San Francisco, and Los Angeles. The immigrant workers are exploited by their own countrymen. As Jewish bosses once sweated Jewish workers and Italians sweated Italians, so nowadays Chinese sweat Chinese. For many Chinese immigrants who end up in the ghetto, the garment sweatshop is the main hope for work.

In New York's Chinatown there are about 350 garment shops. They employ more than 8,000 Chinese to run the presses and sewing machines. This is what an investigative reporter found:

For ten, eleven, sometimes even twelve hours a day, they work under conditions that range from the tolerable to the squalid, earning wages often so low—bringing in some cases less than $50 a week—they approach the closest

*thing we have in this country to a slave-labor system.
[The shops are] in grimy walk-up tenements, converted
apartments, or storefronts, their windows closed to the
scrutiny of the outside world by a coat of gray paint or
soiled sheets hung with tacks. Only the signs posted outside—"Experienced Sewing Machine Operator Needed"
—and the lights that sometimes burn all night indicate
what's going on within.*

The sweatshops all pay piece rates. Women sew
sleeves or shirtfronts for five cents apiece. If they
work furiously, they may make 30 of these—
which adds up to much less than the minimum
wage. A boss may pay as little as one cent a collar.
A hard worker can do 200 collars a day. That's $2
a day in earnings. Many workers take home only
$60 to $75 for working a 50- or 60-hour week.

Such terrible conditions are said to exist in both
union and nonunion shops in America's Chinatowns. It has been hard to get at the facts because
of a wall of silence. The sweatshop system relies
on powerful family and ethnic ties. The immigrant workers see the system as the only way to
get hold of the bottom rung of the economic ladder. It takes a while for them to realize that they
will probably never climb any higher.

In many Chinese restaurants the exploitation is

just as bad. Workers get no overtime pay or health benefits. They put in 12-hour days for as little as 40 cents an hour and tips. When they are sick, they are often required to pay the boss to find a replacement.

One reason there are few unions in America's Chinatowns is that many employees are illegal aliens. They fear they will be reported to the Immigration and Naturalization Service if they try to organize. To complain when they are here illegally would mean risking exposure and deportation. Another reason is that, compared with wages in Hong Kong, pay here seems generous at least—until workers learn what the union scale outside Chinatown is. So they go on, scared of their employers, scared of the government. Nor has organized labor tried to do much for Chinese workers.

What poor pay does, of course, is to make living conditions poor, too. The worst slums in California, says one authority, are in San Francisco's Chinatown.

If the Chinese immigrants who can speak English look for work in the crafts or as skilled laborers, they still meet discrimination. The trade unions often manage to keep the Chinese and other racial minorities out of the skilled trades by one means or another. Often they fail to comply with affirmative action agreements. And government agencies do not do enough to enforce the nondiscrimination laws.

Although some Chinese Americans find work in corporations or in civil service, they are not given these jobs in proportion to their number in the population. Promotion to senior management positions is uncommon. Discrimination is legally barred, but prejudice can operate in indirect ways.

Are Chinese Americans really making it, then?

A higher level of education has not brought the Chinese an income comparable to that of white Americans with the same training. There is no doubt that they are far better off than the Chinese immigrants of the nineteenth century. But more meaningful is comparison to white Americans of today. Discrimination still produces unequal results. The Chinese Americans feel they have to work harder than whites, that they can go only so far in many fields, that a limit is quietly set to their advance. In social life barriers of prejudice, snobbery, and exclusiveness often stand in their way.

The effects of discrimination vary. Some Chinese Americans give up all identification with their ethnic group. The elite who choose assimilation into American society say they find it neither hard nor painful. With the right background, they have no problems. Some go the opposite way. They strongly assert their ethnic heritage and take pride in their uniqueness. They think assimilation is neither possible nor desirable. They reject the image of the stoic, passive Asian who suffers in silence. They fight for what they believe is right. Still others straddle both groups, torn between them.

The integration that was once so much talked of no longer seems to be the issue. What the Chinese Americans and other ethnic and racial groups work for now is an equal chance in life. Some may wish to "join" white society; some may not. But all want a fair share in making the economic and political decisions that determine the quality of everyday life.

Numbers, in this connection, can mean a great deal. There are about 500,000 Chinese Americans; they are only one-fourth of one percent of the total population of the United States. This means they have small influence compared with the 12 percent who are black Americans. The Native Americans are few in number, too. But their possession of lands rich in minerals and oil gives them some bargaining power. When all Americans of Asian origin, who number some two million, unite to work for a better life, their prospects can only improve. And they will improve still more if Asian Americans form alliances with other groups seeking justice and equality.

Bibliography

I AM DEEPLY indebted to the publications of the Chinese Historical Society of America. (It is at 17 Adler Place, San Francisco, California 94133.) Its two publications that I have made greatest use of are listed below. The syllabus, containing bibliographies on all aspects of the subject, will be especially helpful to those who wish to go deeper into Chinese-American history. The other work contains papers given by scholars at a national conference held in 1975.

To the Kraus and McCague books I owe many of the details found in Chapter 2. Professor Stanford M. Lyman's research and writing are indispensable to the understanding of this part of the American past. *Longtime Californ'*, in which Chinese Americans often speak in their own words, gives every reader an intimate sense of history in the making. Stan Steiner's *Fusang,* like all his ethnic studies, is an absorbing account offering many fresh facts and provocative insights.

The sources given here are a selection of the books and articles I referred to in my research.

Billington, Ray Allen. *The Far Western Frontier, 1830–1860.* New York: Harper & Row, Publishers, 1956.

Bulletin of Concerned Asian Scholars. "Asia in America." Special issue, Fall 1972.

Chai, Chu'u, and Chai, Winberg. *The Changing Society of China.* New York: Mentor Books, 1969.

Chinese Historical Society of America. *The Life, Influence and the Role of the Chinese in the United States, 1776–1960.* San Francisco: Chinese Historical Society of America, 1976.

Chinn, Thomas W.; Lai, H. M.; and Choy, P. P., eds. *A History of the Chinese in California: A Syllabus.* San Francisco: Chinese Historical Society of America, 1969.

Chiu, Ping. *Chinese Labor in California: An Economic Study.* Madison: State Historical Society of Wisconsin, 1963.

Council on Interracial Books for Children. *Stereotypes, Distortions and Omissions in U.S. History Textbooks.* New York: Council on Interracial Books for Children, 1977.

Coolidge, Mary R. *Chinese Immigration*. New York: Henry Holt, 1909; New York: Arno Press, 1969.

Fujitomi, Irene, and Wong, Diane. "The New Asian-American Woman." In *Female Psychology: The Emerging Self,* edited by Sue Cox. Chicago: Science Research Associates, 1976.

Daniels, Roger. *The Politics of Prejudice*. Berkeley: University of California Press, 1977.

Daniels, Roger, and Olin, Spencer C., Jr. *Racism in California: A Reader in the History of Oppression*. New York: Macmillan Co., 1972.

Dinnerstein, Leonard, and Reimers, David M. *Ethnic Americans: A History of Immigration and Assimilation*. New York: New York University Press, 1977.

Fairbank, John K. *Chinese-American Interactions: A Historical Summary*. New Brunswick, N. J.: Rutgers University Press, 1975.

————. *The United States and China*. 3rd ed. Cambridge: Harvard University Press, 1972.

Gittings, John. *A Chinese View of China*. New York: Pantheon Books, 1973.

Glazer, Nathan, and Moynihan, Daniel P., eds. *Ethnicity, Theory and Experience*. Cambridge: Harvard University Press, 1975.

Higham, John. *Strangers in the Land*. New York:

Atheneum Publishers, 1963.

Hucker, Charles O. *China to 1850: A Short History*. Palo Alto, Calif.: Stanford University Press, 1978.

Jones, Maldwyn A. *American Immigration*. Chicago: University of Chicago Press, 1960.

Kraus, George. *High Road to Promontory: Building the Central Pacific Across the High Sierra*. San Francisco: American West, 1969.

Lai, H. Mark. *History of the Chinese in America*. San Francisco: Chinese American Studies Planning Group, 1973.

Lan, Dean. *Prestige with Limitations: Realities of the Chinese-American Elite*. San Francisco: R & E Research Associates, 1976.

Lee, Samuel D. "The Chinese Single Man." In *Bulletin of Chinese Historical Society of America*, September 1977.

Lewis, Marvin. *The Mining Frontier*. Norman: University of Oklahoma Press, 1967.

Loewen, James L. *The Mississippi Chinese: Between Black and White*. Cambridge: Harvard University Press, 1971.

Lyman, Stanford M. *The Asian in North America*. Santa Barbara, Calif.: ABC-Clio, 1977.

———*Chinese Americans*. New York: Random House, 1974.

McCague, James. *Moguls and Iron Men: The Story of the First Transcontinental Railroad.* New York: Harper & Row, Publishers, 1964.

McClellan, Robert. *The Heathen Chinee: A Study of American Attitudes Toward China, 1890–1905.* Columbus: Ohio State University Press, 1971.

McWilliams, Carey. *Factories in the Field.* Boston: Little, Brown & Co., 1959.

————. *A Mask for Privilege.* Boston: Little, Brown & Co., 1948.

Mann, Arthur. *Immigrants in American Life.* Boston: Houghton Mifflin Co., 1968.

Melendy, Howard B. *The Oriental Americans.* New York: Twayne Publishers, 1972.

Miller, Stuart C. *The Unwelcome Immigrant: The American Image of the Chinese, 1785–1882.* Berkeley: University of California Press, 1969.

Nee, Victor G., and Nee, Brett de Bary. *Longtime Californ': A Documentary Study of an American Chinatown.* New York: Pantheon Books, 1973.

Saxton, Alexander. *The Indispensable Enemy: Labor and the Anti-Chinese Movement in California.* Berkeley: University of California Press, 1971.

Schulman, Jay; Schatter, Aubrey; and Ehrlich, Rosalie. *Pride and Protest: Ethnic Roots in America.* New York: Dell Publishing Co., 1977.

Steiner, Stan. *Fusang: The Chinese Who Built America.*

New York: Harper & Row, Publishers, 1979.

Tan, Mely Giok-lan. *The Chinese in the U.S.* Taiwan: Orient Cultural Service, 1971.

Wheeler, Thomas C., ed. *The Immigrant Experience.* New York: The Dial Press, 1971.

Wu, Cheng-Tsu. *Chink! Documentary History of Anti-Chinese Prejudice in America.* New York: The World Publishing Company, 1972.

Index